INSF STORIES

FOR YOUNG ATHLETES

A collection of unbelievable stories about mental toughness, courage, self-confidence (Motivational book for girls)

CATHY SUSMAN

Author: Cathy Susman
illustrator: Oriol San Julian - Team of dibustock.com

Table of Contents

INTRODUCTION

Are you ready to check the time on your watch or clock? Guess what time it is? It's *girl power* hour! Join a cast of global, strong, gutsy, and diverse female characters on a journey to become more empowered not only in sports such as tennis, but also in life.

Specifically, you'll read about brave and bold girls just like you who discover key life lessons such as justice, grit, work/school/sports/life balance, resilience, determination, gender equity, an attitude of gratitude, discipline, fairness, perseverance, optimism, anti-bullying messages, dealing with family illness, loss, and bereavement, maintaining a clear focus and concentration, body positivity, breaking stereotypes, self-belief, self-confidence, problem solving skills, the value of teamwork, forgiveness, and other key concepts. Which ones are you eager to investigate?

In addition to discovering essential character education lessons and discerning what's right from what's wrong in your life, school, sports, personal relationships, and family obstacles, you'll not only gain girl power galore but also cultural and geographical information related to renowned and special places such as the Swiss Alps, the Outer Banks, Kentucky, North Carolina, Los Angeles and San Diego, The Florida Keys, Bali, Indonesia, Omaha, Nebraska, California, Arizona, Delaware, England, Massachusetts, Tokyo, Japan, and other memorable settings . Not only will we explore key socioemotional and life skills but also multidisciplinary and multicultural ones to expand our worldviews. Get global with girl power hour as well!

Besides, these stories of strength further ooze with girl power, so *go and glow* with us! They're not only super informative but also engaging, suspenseful, action-packed, thrilling, and interactive. Social justice themes such as gender and racial equity, body image empowerment, socioeconomic justice, mental health matters (depression, fears, and anxiety), and another relevant topics are also presented in a kid and teen-friendly manner.

Go and glow with *girl power for hours* as we splash, climb, throw, row, skate, catch, shoot, and spring with these athletic and awesome female characters. You'll also uncover facts about the world of sports, including mountain climbing, horseback riding and racing (equestrian), swimming, tennis, volleyball, basketball, track and field, softball, figure skating, ballet, etc.

Grab your cozy blanket or favorite spot for unforgettable, engaging, and energetic stories that will give you tons of girl power to last for hours!

CHAPTER 1

Jenna Aces It With Fairness and Justice: A Young Tennis Player Learns Equity

Are you currently struggling to *ace* a test, try a new sport, learn a hobby, master a skill, or pass a difficult school subject? Do you often find yourself questioning what's right from what's wrong in your life, your personal relationships, your choices regarding free time, your athletic ventures, or when stopping patterns that keep you dazed and confused, etc.? Have you been stressed or jaded lately due to gender, socioeconomic class, or other family labels or generational issues? This story will teach how discipline truly precedes success and also celebrates the role of justice, fairness, and equity.

Similarly, this sensational story covers the life of a young tennis athlete named Jenna. This strong, determined girl works hard to make an impact on the world, despite facing unfair circumstances, gender barriers, and other obstacles time and time again.

Read on to determine if young Jenna will change the world of sports and acquire vital life lessons and key character traits related to fairness and justice. Like Jenna, do you see yourself lacking fairness and justice to succeed and persevere in sports, school, friendships, family events, or just life in general? We don't need to be a famous lawyer of a TV judge like Judge Judy in order to comprehend these important lessons.

What's more, we'll travel to many outstanding destinations; for example, the sunny state of California to Beverly Hills, Los Angeles, and other areas, to not only catch some waves but also some tennis points on the court in this savvy story with Jenna as she uncovers how to use fairness and justice to excel in life and in in her beloved sport of tennis. We'll even travel across "the pond" to London, England for even more cultural intersections and relevant life themes.

Ever since birth, it was clear that Jenna was a special and gifted girl. When other babies played with stuffed animals, she used odds and ends around the house and pretended to play tennis with them. She always dreamt of a life filled with purpose and becoming like the famous Williams sisters. So with every step she took, she worked hard, thought positively, and kept an open mind and heart to make her dreams a reality.

Unlike other females her age, who only played dress up and dolls, Jenna loved sports—but she noticed something. Even though she was taught about fairness at a young age, she didn't actually experience it on the tennis court. At the time, tennis was a sport mainly played by only rich people at a fancy country club and mostly men and boys.

At home, Jenna's situation wasn't ideal or smooth while growing up, as her mother had to work two jobs to provide because her father was quite sick. Her mother had to sew her white shorts and even borrow a used tennis racket from Mrs. Mariana, who had previously worked for wealthy people in Beverly hills.

The racket wasn't in good shape, but Jenna made it work either way. It was her first try-out, and her mother drove her to the court, which was miles away from home.

As Jenna grew up, her dad gave her and her brother equal opportunities. Each time they played together, Dad was fair with the pair, but once she arrived at the court, she realized the world doesn't work like that! *It wasn't full of justice and equity!*

The first try-outs were disappointing—obviously no one can be an expert after a few days, so Jenna stayed as positive, disciplined, and practiced as she could.

Her mother was her biggest supporter: she didn't drive Jenna for long hours in hopes that her daughter would one day become a Wimbledon Grand slam champion, saving them from poverty.

Instead, Mom did it because she knew her daughter was the happiest while playing tennis.

Even though during Jenna's first few trials, she didn't exhibit excellent skills because of nervousness, her mother didn't accuse her daughter of not being good enough. In reality, Mom was super supportive throughout her daughter's journey.

Also, that particular evening when Jenna played tennis for the first time sparked, it a special occurrence. She fell in love with the sport even more and aimed to make it her career goal, not just a hobby!

Days passed and Jenna's mother tried to find ways to make her daughter's love for the sport blossom. So, she found a coach; Mr. Smith, who was giving free lessons to children who couldn't afford it.

Since Jenna remained highly disciplined and practiced, her skills were more polished than before, so she managed to impress the coach who agreed to work with her.

Jenna was then scheduled to practice with her serious coach, so she had to find equipment and uniform that was appropriate. For example, she started doing odd jobs such as selling lemonade on a hot day and taking out the neighbor's trash until she saved the right amount of money to buy what she needed.

Once she earned enough money, her mother accompanied her to the sports shop to buy a new racket and white shorts for Jenna. Her daughter was beyond excited and this made her realize that hard work was important if one wanted to achieve a goal.

Soon after, Jenna started practicing with Mr. Smith and entering tournaments, where she learned that being a female tennis player was way harder than she had initially thought.

Working hard during practice and remaining disciplined didn't faze her, since she was getting better with each passing day! Yet what astonished Jenna was the fact that she wasn't getting equal opportunities like the boys at the club. And even though she had started winning consistently, they didn't take her seriously because she was a girl!

On one unforgettable occurrence, they even didn't allow her to be in the group photo, despite the fact that she was the reason why the club had a winner! At such a young age, she didn't understand injustice at all. *How was I the best player in the club but the least appreciated?*

So, she went to her father's room, who was lying on the bed in a sickly state. "Papa, why are the boys in my team more appreciated than me?" She asked in a distressed voice.

"Jenna, I've always given you and your brother equal chances. Sports and life are similar, since they require fair play to succeed," her dad replied.

"But, why do I feel like there's no gender fairness or equity in tennis, especially at the country club?" Jenna asked.

"Some people don't like playing fair, but that shouldn't stop you from fighting for what you want," he patiently explained.

"Some of my teammates don't want to play fair and sometimes I'm not even allowed to play for the club!" Jenna revealed as she started to sob. Her dad consoled her by hugging her.

"You should never let anyone make this feel like you don't deserve what you want!" Jenna's dad reiterated.

"Yes, Papa. How are you feeling?" Jenna asked.

"Better," Her father replied as he coughed.

It was clear that his health was getting worse and the situation at home wasn't good. So, Jenna decided to take part in paid competitions. During the competitions, she noticed that the audience never cheered her on—just her mother and brother.

When she won the competition, she wasn't given a decent pay, but when a boy won the competition, he was rewarded with a lump sum of money. *Things had to change and they had to change fast!*

At the age of 12, it was obvious that Jenna's dream was to play tennis at Wimbledon, London. She wanted to win the championships, so she kept working hard towards achieving her goals. Her talent would only be commended by fellow women or girls her age. And even though she wasn't getting the recognition she deserved, she was happy to represent her gender fiercely on the court.

During a tournament, Jenna further sparked the interest of a special woman who later on took Jenna under her wing by offering to coach her. In other words, Miss Joanne had formerly won 12 grand slam championships and was a top tennis player in the past. Her tactics were excellent and she convinced Jenna that it was possible for a woman to win the championships held at London.

With Miss Joanne, Jenna realized something important: her career as a tennis player was much bigger than she was! If she managed to win those championships, she would be motivating other fellow girls to chase after their dreams of justice, equity, and fairness. She also began winning more games than ever before and moved from the 20th place in Los Angeles to 5th, which was a huge improvement!

Years passed, and she turned 17. Even though Jenna had become an excellent player, her unjust treatment remained the same. Her father died, but his lessons stayed forever. Getting over his death was one of the hardest things she ever did, but he lived on through her. Each time she won a tournament, she dedicated the victory to him. "Jenna, stay on the right path," because her father used to say, "Discipline comes before success."

Her mother and brother remained supportive over the years and never gave up on her. With such a strong family behind her, pushing her towards success, she knew she could conquer any difficulty.

After winning championships in her hometown, she quickly secured victories all over the U.S., which eventually opened her doors to Wimbledon, where she was accompanied by her family and Miss Joanne.

As she arrived in London, she was in shock. Her dream was slowly becoming a reality after so much hard work and sacrifices but the journey was just beginning!

At Wimbledon, she played with a girl, and they won the women's double title, making them the youngest team to ever do it. But since they were women, they didn't make it to the news headlines like the winners of the men's double title tended to achieve.

The industry wasn't changing, even though Jenna was getting older and becoming more victorious. Each time she would bring it up, Miss Joanne would tell her that was the way the world worked, but Jenna knew she had to fight for change, justice, and equality. *Tennis wasn't just for men—it was a game everyone could enjoy!*

So, she decided to practice harder than any other player. She thought that if she won more championships, she would get the respect she deserved, but she was wrong.

After the biggest highlight of her career; winning the second time in Wimbledon, she was interviewed by reporters. It was a small improvement, and so she arrived at the newsroom ahead of interview time. The reporters were an hour late and during the interview, and they didn't ask her about the sport. Instead, they posed irrelevant questions, which made her leave the room in fury.

Despite winning so many championships, she was still not getting the respect a winner of her tennis caliber deserved. If she was a man with her achievements, the world would deem Jenna as *Superman*! So, she knew she had to take action immediately and formed an organization for female athletes, where they would spark a conversation about the equality in sports. Their motto was *Fair Play, Fair Victory.*

At the organization, she was able to meet different athletes from different sports who explained the unfair situation in the sports world.

They decided to protest against the unfairness in the sports world but nobody was willing to listen. As time went by, Jenna started feeling like her victories meant nothing so she visited her mother, "Mother, why do I feel so empty after all these victories?" She asked.

"Just because others don't want to see your talent doesn't mean you should look at your precious achievements through the eyes of people who don't understand the importance of virtues such as fairness, justice, equity, and discipline," her mother explained.

"But..." Even before Jenna could finish her sentence, her mother intervened, "I raised you to see yourself and others through the eyes of love. You don't need the world's validation, just your own. You're playing tennis because it makes you happy, have you forgotten?" Mother asked.

"No, I..."

"The world is changing, Jenna. Soon, they'll see how special you are, but you must remain disciplined. Your purpose is bigger than you are!" Jenna's mother added.

She left her mother's house feeling at peace with herself. Her mother had just given her clarity and Jenna knew what her next steps would be: with the money she had earned through hard work, she started spreading valuable information about women in sports after buying a news corporation, which would interview female athletes and showcase sports which women took part in equally. If no one was willing to make a change, she had to rise up to the challenge and spearhead the changes that would impact the next generation of women athletes.

All in all, Jenna's efforts to highlight the talents of women in sports was starting to gain momentum and she began seeing profound changes in the sports industry.

After winning a championship, she would be interviewed by reporters in a respectful manner. Her payment started increasing and even though it wasn't the same level as the male tennis players, she knew that if she kept spreading awareness, it would soon be.

Then her name was on most people's tongue and schools started reporting that more girls started joining sports teams. The impact was much bigger than she had hoped and this was much better than winning the championships—she was changing people's lives and instilling justice and equity!

Miss Joanne was proud of her and even though it was time for her to retire, she was glad that her student was doing something much bigger than any other athlete.

Jenna eventually opened a sports center for young girls who wanted to be coached but didn't have enough money. Thousands flooded the gate during the try-outs, which was a clear sign that the world of sports was changing rapidly. Her accomplishments weren't just her own; she was sharing them with others!

Jenna's family was proud of the impact she was making—especially her mother who had been there for her since the first day when Jenna held a racket. It was a long journey, but she was happy that her daughter had finally made her dreams a reality.

All in all, Jenna became a beacon of women's sports and her efforts paved the way for other female athletes overall, not just in tennis. She was eventually given the respect and recognition she deserved after remaining disciplined and working hard towards fulfilling an important cause for justice and gender equity in sports. Her life's purpose yielded so many opportunities for others.

Learned lessons

As demonstrated in this superb story, the unfairness of the world shouldn't shun ever you from your dreams, goals, desires, and objectives. Just because the world refuses to acknowledge you based on income, race, gender, culture, language, special needs, or weight doesn't mean you should stop acknowledging your own efforts or quit affirming gender equity, justice, and discipline in all that you do.

All in all, ***Jenna Aces It With Fairness and Justice: A Young Tennis Player Learns Equity*** reminds us to persevere with fair, focus, determination, and advocacy, regardless of what we seek to pursue in life, school, hobbies, home, sports, or friendships.

Always remember how Jenna overcame family socioeconomic stress in the form of her father's death, poverty, and gender barriers when you felt like giving up due to some injustices around you as this tale highlights how discipline truly precedes success and also celebrates the role of gender justice, fairness, and equity in our lives.

It's now your turn to ace it with practical applications and post-reading activities to extend and apply your learning!

1. Mirror, Mirror: Draw a mirror and label it with words to describe Jenna. Glow with grammar as you use adjectives and nouns such as winner, advocate, determined, equitable, for example.

2. Movie Mania: Discuss a song, cartoon, movie, or book that addresses the lack of fairness and justice in sports, school, friendships, family events, or just life in general?

3. California Dreaming: Locate Beverly Hills and Los Angeles on a map of California. What other landmarks do you notice?

4. Dear Daddy: Imagine you are Jenna at age 40. Write a letter to her father about the life lessons he taught her about justice, determination, gender equity, etc.

5. Cali Cool: With a parent's permission, go online and locate 2-4 fun facts about the state bird, motto, flower, history, main industries, population, etc.

CHAPTER 2

Demi's Dream: An Aquatic Tale of Resilience and Perseverance

*I*n order to win in life, you need to always stay focused, positive, and rise to the challenge. Do you ever feel like a fish out of water as you try to stay focused on a goal or dream? As this story showcases, you should persevere through the difficulties you face and remain resilient just like Demi.

As a result, this aquatic, action-packed tale as it closely follows a young swimmer who must pass through challenging odds to achieve her athletic and life dreams. Like a mermaid's tail, Demi models for readers that resilience and perseverance can serve as a lifeboat to enable us to *float through life, overcome obstacles, defy the odds, and make a big splash as women and girls.*

Practice holding your breath because we'll venture under and above water as Demi swiftly discovers why never quitting is an essential part of resilience and persevere in pursuit of one's goals, hopes, dreams, and aspirations, both in sports and in life as a whole. We'll also address issues of bullying and family support.

Demi allowed the waves to lift her up. Even though others feared the sea—she was fascinated by it and it held no anxiety for her. On the contrary, it gave her a sense of unimaginable peace, bliss, and clarity. She swam back to the shore and ran barefoot on the rough sand back home. The ocean breeze blew towards her, making her midnight black hair blow in the wind, giving her a soothing sensation.

Her grandmother, Aurora, also loved the sea. Grandma's fierce nature allowed her to sail around the world. When Demi was born, her grandma came back to the water town they were living in near Boston, Massachusetts, USA. Before Demi could walk, her grandmother taught her how to swim like a fish.

She then inherited her grandmother's brave nature and deep love for water. In Boston's main square, people would spread rumors that the women in Demi's family were *half human half mermaid*, so that was why they enjoyed the water so much and even swam in the midst of gigantic waves during rough weather conditions.

At school, local kids viewed Demi as quite peculiar. She used to dive in the swimming pool every chance she got, even during the cold winter weather, yet she never suffered from any flu, dry skin, or colds. It was as if she had made a pact with water and it agreed to never harm her.

She had one friend named Flora and they were inseparable. "Did you hear what the kids are saying?" Flora asked.

"Flo, you know I don't care!" Demi insisted.

"But…" Flora hesitated.

"But, what?" Demi asked.

"They think you're a superhuman, like a mermaid or something," Flora replied.

Demi let out a hysterical laugh, making everyone in the room stare at her. "The swimming championships will commence soon, I don't have the time to listen to false and silly rumors," Demi giggled and the bell immediately rang.

It was time for swimming practice, so she went to the locker room to change into her swimsuit. Everyone else had arrived, except her. Miss Rory was always rude to Demi, despite Demi winning so many games.

"And, where were you, Demi?" She barked.

"I was still in class, the lesson just ended," Demi politely replied.

"Just because others think you're a good swimmer doesn't mean I do! Your tardiness speaks volumes. BENCH!" Miss Rory shouted.

Even though Demi had won the previous championships, Miss Rory made it hard for her throughout the school year. It was as though the coach had some sort of personal *vendetta* against Demi.

"But, I can't sit on the bench while others are practicing!" Demi argued.

"Demi, to the principal's office…NOW!" Miss Rory remarked.

The whole team stood and watched in silence as Demi was unfairly sent away, despite being the best swimmer in the team.

"She literally hates me!" Demi insisted.

"You'll have to bring your parents tomorrow!" Principal Perry said.

"My parents are away on business, so I currently live with my grandmother," Demi explained.

"You can ask her to come," the principal stated.

Demi was disappointed: she didn't understand why Miss Rory always found a way to make her life miserable.

At home, she couldn't find her grandmother, and so she went to look for her where she knew she'd find her—the beach.

Aurora was a free-spirit and had just come back from surfing. She was also pretty young for her age, so her body could still function properly, if not better than most youngsters. She was stronger than an ox; mentally and physically.

"Sweeting, aren't you supposed to be at school?" Aurora asked.

"It's my swimming coach!" Demi replied.

"Again?" Aurora asked in disbelief.

"Yes, I was late for practice since the previous teacher didn't leave on time and so, she decided to punish me. But I defended myself, and it landed me in trouble," Demi explained.

"Honey, why's that coach always on your case?" Aurora asked.

"I don't know, Grandma," Demi replied.

"You'll have to accompany me to school to talk to the Principal Perry and Miss Rory," she added.

"Alright, honey! Now cheer up! It'll be fine. Clearly, this coach has something against you, and I'd like to know why!" Aurora insisted.

The next day, Demi woke up and prepared to go to school. Aurora accompanied her, and they arrived on time at the principal's office where Miss Rory was waiting for them as well.

"Did Demi inform you about yesterday's occurrence?" Miss Rory asked.

"Yes, but I'd like to hear it from your perspective," Aurora replied as she stared Miss Rory straight in her eyes without blinking, making her look away.

"Tell me, what did my girl do? Because as far as I'm concerned, you've been making her life difficult throughout practice," Aurora stated while still maintaining eye contact.

"She arrived late to practice and talked back to me," Miss Rory explained.

"So, what have you decided?" Aurora asked.

"We've chosen to remove her from the swimming team!" Principal Perry announced.

"Isn't that punishment a bit too harsh? She's the best swimmer in school!" Aurora argued.

"Her lack of discipline is in question," Miss Rory remarked.

At this point, Demi is shock as questions cloud her mind. *How will I now become the best swimmer in the Boston region? Where will I practice? Why would this woman cut my dreams short out of malice?*

Without saying anything, Demi burst out of the room in tears.

"You just threw away a girl's dream just because you felt like it? Are you happy now?" Aurora declared as she followed behind Demi.

Miss Rory stood in the office, showing no remorse or compassion.

"We'll find a way, my girl. When life throws you lemons, you must make a delicious glass of lemonade," Aurora consoled Demi, but it was impossible. During the next few days, Demi couldn't talk. She also had trouble eating—her dreams were abruptly taken from her.

"Demi, you're much stronger than this. You've been persevering for a long time. You're very disciplined and with the willingness to find a way to fight for your dreams, you'll realize nobody can take them away from you!" Aurora explained.

After hearing those words, Demi spoke for the first time in two weeks, "I'm hungry, Nana." While she only uttered a few words, it gave her grandmother hope that Demi would soon resume back to normal determined and cheerful self.

As a result, Demi returned to her classes, even though going to the pool area made her terribly sad. Her classmates, who had previously thought that she was peculiar, realized that she was only passionate about swimming, so they were now supportive during this hard time.

Flora tried to find solutions to help her best friend return to swimming. For example, she even made a flyer, which contained information about a swimming gala.

"Hey, it's not huge, but you never know. It might open endless opportunities," Flora insisted.

"I'll try it! Thank you, my friend," Demi remarked.

The gala was looking for talented swimmers who would participate in a paid competition. Even though the reward wasn't much in terms of monetary amount, Demi decided to attend the try-outs. She was accompanied by her grandmother, Aurora, and her best friend, Flora.

During the try-outs, it was clear that Demi would win the competition easily because she surpassed the other swimmers by a long distance. She was eventually picked and won the top prize.

This prompted her to be approached by a talented woman who offered to coach her because Demi's talent was unmatched. Each Saturday, Demi would practice with Miss Lorelai and her new coach's impact was so profound, that Demi started winning accolades more than ever, moving from county galas to regional tournaments, where competition grew harder because most swimmers were serious and had been practicing their whole lives.

Still, Demi remained disciplined and resilient. She persevered and practiced harder than ever with Miss Lorelai. Demi's name became renowned in Boston's swimming world, and this fame made Miss Rory angry. Miss Rory had been sabotaging Demi's efforts for years and thought that she'd sever Demi's final chances of being a swimmer once and for all, but that didn't happen. Demi persevered, focused, and remained resilient.

However. Miss Rory started thinking of a plan to end Demi's career for good.

In the meantime, Demi was practicing hard with Miss Lorelai, who made her see things from a different perspective. For the first time in her life, Demi felt that her dreams were closer than ever, but she knew she just had to practice harder and become much more disciplined.

During the regionals, Demi wasn't able to collect as many trophies as she had during the county level. However, the lessons she obtain were still worth it. First, she discovered so much by competing with some of the most talented swimmers who were also on their personal journeys to become the best swimmers the world had ever seen.

"These people aren't your enemies; they're just your opponents in the water. Outside the water, there's so much you can learn from them," Miss Lorelai advised.

Based on Miss Lorelai's mentorship and coaching, Demi had developed a sharp mentality, which made her mindset much more mature than her peers.

Since Demi was becoming popular in the state's swimming world, Boston's Swimmer's Association asked her school why Demi wasn't on the swimming team and urged them to take her back as soon as possible.

Miss Rory was unhappy with the Association's decision and hatched a plan as soon as possible. Even when she tried to explain that Demi wasn't disciplined or respectful, the Association insisted that Demi was one of the most talented and integral swimmers they'd ever encountered.

The leader of the association asked whether the principal conducted a thorough investigation before kicking her out, but he confirmed that there wasn't an investigation.

Once Principal Perry conducted an investigation, he noticed that the other swimmers insisted that Miss Rory was making it hard for Demi and eventually the coach was fired. Even though the school swimming team asked Demi to join them once again, she declined because her busy schedule wouldn't permit it.

She kept practicing with Miss Lorelai instead and soon Demi ranked among the few swimmers who moved to the national level.

When the news spread across Boston, everyone was pleased—except Miss Rory. She decided to call Demi to apologize, but she had yet another a plan to ruin the young girl.

Since Demi didn't understand why Miss Rory was so hostile towards her, Demi naively decided to go to her home.

"Welcome Demi, Thank you for taking your precious time to see me," Miss Rory grimaced.

Demi then remained quiet, waiting to hear what the former coach had to say.

"You silly little girl! You thought I called you to apologize?" Miss Rory hissed in a pretentious tone.

"You're the reason why Caleb left me: to take care of you and your mother," she added.

Demi was in shock, because she couldn't believe Miss Rory was so malicious because of events Demi personally had no control over.

Suddenly, Miss Rory dragged Demi to a room and locked it as Demi was screaming loudly for help.

"You'll never leave! So, since you'll miss the national championships tomorrow, your dream won't come into fruition!" Miss Rory bellowed.

At this point, Demi knew that screaming for help or begging Miss Rory to let her out wouldn't yield any results, so Demi started to think with resilience, determination, and persistence.

The room she was locked in had no windows to escape, but it had a duct on the ceiling. Since she was athletic, Demi found her way out of the house and rushed to the police to report Miss Rory who was eventually arrested.

Demi's grandmother stayed with her all night and hoped she wouldn't break down. Contrary to her expectations, Demi remained strong and was ready for the national championships that would be held the next day.

The sun glistened brightly, waking them up for the critical occasion. Demi prepared for the match that would be held at her school, which had never occurred before in Boston's history.

The audience was filled with her classmates, Flora, Aurora, and her parents who flew back from business to watch her. The support Demi received pushed her to perform well during the competition. And even though her opponents were professionals, Demi was able to secure the win, making herself, her grandma, her coach, her parents, and her city of Boston proud.

Learned lessons

As Demi's resilient story clearly represented, we must never give up on our goals, dreams, hopes, and aspirations in life, school, sports, or social contexts. We can also rely on help from relatives, supportive school staff, and coaches, as Demi did.

With perseverance as your wings (or fins in Demi's case!), you can soar and succeed over anything that you set your mind toward achieving. The difficulties you face shouldn't determine your future. You can use the obstacles or challenges as fuel to excel.

Just as Demi modelled, it's vital ton always find another way to achieve your goals, even though the path may seem hidden, impossible, or blocked. Once a door closes, embrace the resilience and persevere because another one will open!

It's now your turn to dive deep with engaging and fun post-reading activities to practice the story's lessons.

1. Poetic Pal: Using the first letter of each word in Demi's name, describe her in the form of an acrostic poem. For example,

Dedication

Energetic

Mindful

Intelligent

2. Screen Time: If you made an app about perseverance and resilience, how would this app work? Why would kids and teens like it?

3. Massachusetts Memories: Locate Boston and Massachusetts on a U. S. map. Which bodies of water do you notice? Which states border it?

4. Dear Nana: Write a thank you note to Demi's grandma about the valuable lessons she provided.

5. Massachusetts Mission: With a parent's permission, go online and locate 2-4 fun facts about the state's history to present. What is the state known for?

CHAPTER 3

Rise Like a Phoenix and Balance Like A Yin/Yang Symbol: Vivian The Volleyball Victor

Are you ready to spread your wings like a beautiful bird? Well, this tale set in the desert city of Mesa, Arizona, USA, uses the iconic symbol of a phoenix to cleverly depict how a brave girl named Vivian soars above strife and rises from the ashes of defeat and failure in her beloved sport of volleyball as well as in life.

In sum, Vivian learns the value of gaining the grit not to quit as she mindfully discovers how to balance her education/social/sports/family life and how to bounce back after failure or adversity.

Similar to the Asian yin/yang symbol, life is all about balance: balanced meals, balanced home/school/sports life, balanced friendships, balanced academic, physical, socioemotional, spiritual, psychological, socioeconomic, and physical health, for example.

As you embark on this cool journey of literacy, love, laughter, and life lessons related to character education traits, let's SPIKE the ball against failures, mistakes, and setbacks as futile and embrace the notion that victories are indeed possible after failures, as Vivian showcases so clearly in today's tale.

It was a hot summer day in the desert city of Mesa, Arizona, USA, as Vivian, a volleyball fanatic, dashed to the backyard, holding a volleyball firmly.

"One game and then we call it a day?" She suggested, while looking at her father; Mr. Wong who was shirtless, enjoying the breeze under a palm tree.

"Viv, it's way too hot," he responded.

"Since when did a hot day prevent you from playing volleyball?" Vivian teased.

"Alright! One game and I'll go back to enjoy the breeze! It's such a hot day," he insisted.

The pair played volleyball anywhere they could find space, as long as they had the ball, the net, and the will.

For example, they played at the beach, the local court, and their backyard. Vivian had shown interest in the sport ever since she could walk, so her parents built a net and bought her balls to play with in their backyard. Whenever she was free, she'd go to the backyard or the beach to play with other kids.

On that day, even though Mr. Wong had said he'd only play one game, they ended up playing until the sun fell away and darkness covered the land with a thick black blanket.

"It's time for dinner," Mrs. Wong summoned the pair. "You two never stop, she playfully added.

As time passed, it was clear that their daughter was destined for great success at volleyball. Even at her young age, her skills were unmatched and Vivian always led her team to victory by scoring numerous goals.

She was a creative soul and found ways to implement new strategies and techniques to her volleyball toolbox, which made her special.

"School starts next week, will you sign up for the volleyball team?" Mrs. Wong inquired.

"Yes! I think it's a good idea," Vivian replied.

"I just hope you'll still focus on your studies," Mrs Wong added.

"Don't worry, Mom!" Vivian assured her as she sprinted to her room.

Mr. Wong was artistic and his daughter's biggest supporter. He gave her space to grow and explore her creative side. But, Mrs. Wong was stricter, so like the yin/yang symbol of their Chinese American culture, she brought balance to her daughter's life, which was equally important.

As much as she was passionate about volleyball, Vivian was also equally one of the best students in school, but she initially lacked school/sports balance.

However, all she ever wanted was to play volleyball at the national championships and that made her stray away from her studies from time to time, but her mother led her back to the right path time and time again.

Days passed and school commenced. Mrs. Wong dropped her at school. It was Vivian's final year at school and she wanted to leave a mark while balancing other responsibilities.

During the previous year, she quit the volleyball team because her grades were suffering, but she promised her mother that this time she would practice balance and ensure that she'd succeed in both schoolwork and volleyball.

School hours ended pretty quickly, so she went to the coach's office.

"Mr. Rahim, I'm certain I can make it work this year. Besides, I've been practicing all summer," she insisted.

"I know how talented you are. The team hasn't been the same ever since you left, but I'm not sure whether your mother will support this decision," he earnestly replied.

"She supports it," Dory assured. "Are you sure?" Mr. Rahim asked, "You can counter check to see if I'm telling you the truth," Dory responds.

"I'm not doubting your integrity, because you're a gifted, talented, and honest girl. I just hope you'll be able to balance practice and school work since it's your last year at school!" Mr. Rahim explained.

"So, I'm in?" She asked excitedly.

"Yes, there's always space for our top player!" Mr. Rahim remarked.

In turn, Vivian was super glad that she was allowed back into the team. At home, she told her parents the excellent news. They were thrilled but reminded her to work hard in school.

Practice commenced after school. Vivian expected the process to be simple, but the coach had changed their strategy and she had to learn the new techniques quickly. There was a steep learning curve: balancing school and volleyball practice was proving to be harder than she had anticipated.

"Coach, I'm having trouble catching up with the new techniques," she admitted.

"Well, you've always been one of my best players. You can get the hang of it as long as you put your head in the game! You can choose to accept the challenge presented to you, or, you can fold and choose to quit," Mr. Rahim stated.

His words stung her and as she was walking home, she went to the beach to relax to find clarity. Yet she didn't understand why balancing work and school was hard. Just last term, she had been crashing it at both until she started giving volleyball all her attention and then began failing at school and grades, making her mother intervene.

After watching the waves crash, she went back home, finished her homework, ate dinner, and went to bed.

That night, she couldn't sleep an inch. The next day, as her father drove her to school, she presented her dilemma, hoping he'd solve it for her.

"What can I say, Viv, you're creative enough, you'll find a solution. Just don't run away from one thing when it gets tough like you did last time. Rise up to the challenge! You can do anything," Mr. Wong remarked.

So, I tend to run away when things get rough?

That evening, during practice, while other girls were paying easily. She was finding it hard until she remembered what her Dad had advised, so she rose to the challenge by creating a new move that allowed her to score for her team during the friendly match at the court.

This motivated her to master the new strategy. If she could create her own moves, she could also learn. The next day, she woke up early and peddled her bike to school. She went to the volleyball court and started practicing the coach's strategy.

Shortly after, it became a common occurrence and she'd arrive at school earlier than everyone else just to practice. Furthermore, this gave her time to focus on her studies, as she'd promised her mother.

After a few weeks, her hard work started paying off! She mastered the new strategy and was creating a new approach of her own to present to the coach. Her new strategy would make Mr. Rahim's strategy yield a better chance at winning the championships, even though they had to work their way up from county level.

Days later, she finished creating the strategy and presented it to Mr. Rahim, who was thrilled to add it to his own coaching resources. Due to her passionate nature and willingness to learn and create new moves and techniques, Vivian was eventually promoted as team captain.

"Your grades are up and you're the team captain! It's time to celebrate, Viv," Mrs. Wong voiced. She was thrilled that her daughter was balancing school, sports, and other responsibilities effortlessly, even though it was hard before.

"So, what's next?" Mr. Wong asked.

"The championships begin next week and we commence at county level," she replied.

The family of three went to celebrate the small wins at a restaurant. Mr. and Mrs. Wong were extremely proud of their daughter and her ability to learn from mistakes.

Vivian further maintained her willingness to learn new things. As much as she was passionate at creating new strategies for her team, she was also focused on school/sports/life balance.

They practiced all week and it was finally the day of the county championships. While it wasn't a big game, it was a good start that would make way for bigger tournaments, so the team gave it their all and won instantaneously.

"Don't let this victory overshadow your mind; it's just the beginning and the next teams you face will require more skill and teamwork," Mr. Rahim explained to the girls as they were celebrating.

His grounded nature always intrigued her. Mr. Rahim kept composure each time and he was right. In order to win, they had to keep at it consistently, balance effectively, and not let a single victory make them overconfident.

So, the next day, the girls showed up for practice and worked harder than ever to prepare for the regional games. This time, Vivian showed them her new moves, and the girls were thrilled to learn!

On a starry night, she sat on the balcony and watched the stars. Footsteps approached the balcony and she felt someone sit next to her, "Tell me, what are you thinking about?" Mrs. Wong asked.

"About school and volleyball," Vivian admitted.

"You know, most people tend to focus on one or the other, but your hobby of volleyball is equally important," Mrs. Wong emphasized.

"But, Mama, volleyball isn't just a hobby. I want to be a professional player," she declared.

"I hear you and you can do anything you set your mind on but education is important as well. I'm so proud of you," Mrs. Wong assured as they both shared a warm embrace.

The following days were filled with so much practice and volleyball/school balance. Mr. Rahim's goal wasn't the national championships; on the contrary, it was to train a group of young girls who would eventually impact the world positively through sports and life lessons, even though they didn't know it.

As much as he trained them to physically win, he also encouraged them to think like winners. He knew that having a clear mindset was important to succeed in life.

In a few weeks, they'd compete at the regional championships, so they prepared until the due date arrived. The court flocked with different faces. The audience was larger than the one from county level. Once the opponents arrived, it was time to start playing.

Even though the previous game was easy—this wasn't. It was the ticket to playing at national level and both teams fought tooth and nail for the spot. At first, it was clear that the opponents would win the Mesa regional championships because they were incredibly good. Even after practicing hard over the weeks, Vivian felt like they weren't as skilled as the other team.

Before the break, the opponents were dominating the match but once the teams resumed playing, Vivian started creating moves to score points. Her teammates also started using the techniques

Mr. Rahim had taught them, and they ended up victorious, even though their chance at winning the game was seemingly thin.

This victory was worth a celebration because they were going to the finals and they won a challenging tournament. They all went to a local restaurant and Mr. Rahim bought them mango slushies.

Since the school year was almost coming to an end, Vivian was under so much pressure. She had to study for her final exams while practicing for the national championships. This was the point in her life that would eventually determine who she'd be. *She had two options: to rise up to the challenge or quit.*

However, after the life lessons she had learnt during that year, she decided to work hard towards her goals. She was certain that she wanted to play volleyball, but she also wanted to get a scholarship to a reputable university and graduate as her mother wanted.

During this final lap, she gave it her all in both areas of her life. She targeted balance. She sat for her final exams and eventually earned a spot at the national championships. While there, dozens of people flooded the court. Her parents attended to support her as well. This time, the team had decided to dominate the game from the beginning and so they did until the second half when the opponents gave them a hard time.

The game was supposed to end early, but since neither of the teams had scored 15 points, it went on longer than expected. Both teams were starting to get tired because neither of them had reached the final mark. That's when Vivian devised a strategy on the pitch and started by passing the ball to players, which the other team didn't expect to score. They anticipated that Vivian would score because she was the captain, so they were blocking her goals on purpose.

As a result of this strategy, the team and Vivian *rose like a phoenix* as they scored a variety of goals until the opponent's team caught up with the tactic and now they started looking out for everyone else on the team, except Vivian. So and that's when she took the opportunity to seal their victory.

The crowd cheered and Mr. and Mrs. Wong told Vivian how proud they were. The results of the final exams came out and Vivian passed with flying colors, earning her spots at top universities. She still pursued volleyball, especially since an agent attended the national games and who eventually took her under his wing.

Learned lessons

Now that you've earned your phoenix wings, are you ready to apply the lessons of determination, school/sports/life balance and discipline in your own life, sports goals, and friendships? When you utilize these important character traits, you'll soon be able to fulfill any goals that you dream. The sky is truly the limit for you, so you can

Soar above strife and rises from the ashes of mistakes, fear, anxiety, defeat, or setbacks, as Vivian mastered in today's terrific tale.

Likewise, let's engage in some fun post-reading activities to further extend our learning:

1. Mesa Magic: Find Mesa, Arizona, USA on a map. What do you notice about the state? Record 2-4 observations to practice geographical skills.

2. Bird Up: Since this story uses the iconic symbol of a phoenix bird to show how we can soar above strife and rise from the ashes of defeat and failure in our lives, draw yourself as a phoenix. Be creative and colorful!

3. Grit and Gumption: Reflect on a time when you exhibited the grit and gumption not to quit as obstacles tried to block your path. How did you overcome fears or setbacks? Explain.

4. Volleyball Legends: With a grownup's permission, go online or check out a book from the local library about 2-4 volleyball legends, living or decreased. Jot down some fun facts about each icon.

5. Asian yin/yang symbol: Expand your own cultural knowledge and re-create what the Asian yin/yang symbol looks like. How does this life philosophy apply to your own beliefs, lifestyle, and personality?

CHAPTER 4

A Sporty Shorty: Shayla Shatters Height Stereotypes and Breaks Records

S hayla is always the shortest girl in class, but she desperately wants to play basketball. Her teammates are making it hard for her since they don't think she's cut out for basketball due to her physical limitation. Will she be able to prove them wrong? Do you want a sensational story that really slam dunks and combats any excuses or obstacles?

Cheer along for Shayla in the lovely Outer Banks of North Carolina, USA, as she tries to break height stereotypes and gender barriers. You'll uncover that we can shatter stereotypes and limitations that others impose on us and we can excel at our goals and even break records, not only in basketball, as Shayla aspired to achieve, but also in school, life, friendship, family, etc. Let's hit a jump shot with this adventurous tale of tenacity and hope.

Shayla was the shortest girl in school with an approximate height of 4"7 feet. Despite her short physique, she still wanted to play basketball. It had been her lifelong dream ever since she saw her older brother play. You might even say that it was in her blood since she resided in the lovely Outer Banks of North Carolina, USA, a state that loves its basketball teams!

But each time she brought it up, it would stir up laughter from the girls on the basketball team. "Sorry, we aren't looking for new mini members," they'd chuckle. "Perhaps, next time," they added with snickers.

Each time, they brushed her off so, Shalya decided to seek out the coach.

"Mr. Colby, I'd really like to join the basketball team, but they won't let me," she explained.

"Why not? You know, there's an extra spot that needs to be filled as soon as possible," Mr. Colby informed.

"When can I try out for the spot," Shayla asked. "

"Well, it needs to be filled immediately, so if you're free right now, it'd be perfect," Mr. Colby confirmed.

"Alright! I was born ready. I'll be at the court in 5 minutes," she cheered as she dashed to the locker room and sported a jersey and some shorts.

As she sprinted along the court, one of the girls barked, "We already told you the spot is taken!"

"By who?" Mr. Colby asked sternly. The girl didn't have a response because the spot wasn't filled.

"Shayla, show me your best court moves!" Mr. Colby urged as he paid close attention.

She started dribbling the ball and scored goals consecutively. Despite her short physique, she'd been practicing with her brother for years and mastered his techniques and skills.

The whole team was in shock! They couldn't believe how rude they'd been to Shayla, yet she was a phenomenal player.

"Now that's talent! You're on the team, Shayla!" Mr. Colby expressed as he walked away. She just couldn't believe her ears!

Finally, she was on the local Outer Banks' basketball team and embarking on a journey towards becoming a top basketball player in the U.S. However, some girls weren't happy with the coach's decision, but they weren't serious players. The school was filled with rich girls who took everything they had for granted.

Shayla had just joined the school through a scholarship a month ago and the girls always treated her like an unwelcome guest. Her parents couldn't afford such an expensive school, but they were happy when she was chosen. Since she didn't come from a rich family, most girls ignored Shayla and labelled her as a small town girl who was too low for their own high standards, except Josie, who was kind to her since the first day of school.

During basketball practice, other teammates laughed at her when they found out that Shayla's previous school in rural Greensboro didn't have a court.

"If she has never played basketball before, then how can she be a valuable addition to the team," Stacy argued.

"Don't be mean, Stacy, we offer equal opportunities to each student in this school. Besides, she's already proven she's an excellent player," Mr. Colby insisted.

"But—she's also soooooooo short!" Stacy added.

"We don't stereotype others based on height, weight, or looks, or body shame others. I'd like to remind you this school doesn't take bullying lightly. Everyone, 10 laps starting now!" Coach Colby instructed.

The girls on the team made faces to show how they were displeased by the coach's decision. These players didn't know that Shayla was very optimistic, resilient, and took each challenge very seriously. She was competitive in nature and rarely gave up until she got her desired results.

During the 10 laps, she earned first place and scored more goals than anyone else during practice, which agitated the other mean girls even more.

"Shayla, great work! Instead of complaining about the new girl, perhaps, you should all try to be like her," the coach suggested.

Shayla was touched by the coach's remarks, so she remained positive and worked hard. Those girls' mean and bullying efforts weren't strong enough to throw her off. She clearly understood that her purpose was bigger than any difficulty that presented itself on her path. She knew she'd overcome body shaming and shatter all stereotypes.

As the days went by, she used to find time to practice basketball, remembering her mother's words, "Practice makes perfect!"

Since she was shining during practice, it motivated other girls to defeat her, so everyone was willing to put in the work. Even though their results weren't as good as Shayla, the coach was glad that at least the members were working hard, which was a rare occurrence.

The team had never won a tournament before and this time there was a glimpse of hope finally. Shayla kept perfecting her passes and techniques. Even during friendly matches when the girls would sneak mean comments, it didn't faze her, which made them wonder why they couldn't put her down. She was too *strong and resilient*!

A month later, it was finally time for the inter-school basketball championships. Shayla had been practicing harder than ever—she wanted to leave a profound mark during the game, so the other girls would respect her. She further wanted to represent shorter girls and show that they also could excel in this sport where height normally mattered.

The teams arrived at the court, ready to compete for the trophy. As the game commenced, it was crystal clear that the team was being dominated by the opposition team. The first half didn't go as they planned and instead of listening to the coach, they started pinning the blame on Shayla.

"She had the chance to score a goal but couldn't! Her buttery hands and Smurf size can't even hold a ball firmly," Stacy argued.

"She's way too nice on the court; she can only handle friendly tournaments. She's too delicate for competitive games," Stacy's friend added.

"Enough! I need you girls to play as a team! This hostility towards Shayla needs to end immediately!" Mr. Colby declared.

The game commenced and this time, Shayla decided to prove her teammates wrong and so as soon as she got hold of the ball, she dribbled it and ran as fast as she could. Her short physicality allowed her to pass through the rival's defense effortlessly, scoring a goal. She was also substantial in creating a good pass for her teammate who was able to score.

They only needed a goal to seal their victory and they were racing against time. So, Shayla decided to go all in, scoring their final game point. They were crowned the winners and next they would participate in a game at a regional level. A former basketball champion presented them the trophy and hugged Shayla since she had contributed so much to winning the game.

After leading the team to winning their first game in years, Shayla became a school celebrity in the Outer Banks and everyone wanted to be friends with her. The other girls' hostility also had reduced so much.

Winning the match gave her a boost of confidence, prompting her to believe in her dreams. She wanted to make a major impact on the school's basketball team, so she practiced harder than ever before. Each chance she got, she spent it at the court, perfecting her skills.

Coach was able to see how good she was getting at making passes, defense and offense, making him promote her to captain. It was clear that Shayla was passionate about the sport and everyone loved to watch her play. Even during practice, they surrounded the court during free periods just to admire her exceptional play.

Her skills were getting better with each passing day and her teammates began valuing her. They started to see that she was a valuable addition. Ever since she joined the team, everyone had started working harder than before and they even won a tournament!

Eventually, the regional competitions started and the team attended the nearby tournament to fight tooth and nail for their spot in the national championships.

At the regional level, they got to meet amazing players who showed excellent sportsmanship skills. As much as they were there to win, they also

took the opportunity as a learning experience because some of the teams would end up at the national level.

The game commenced and since they practiced team work unlike the first match, they won the game easily. The audience cheered as the winners received their rewards. The next stop was the national championships.

The following day, Shayla and her mother decided to go out to catch up since she was busy working most of the time and they rarely had time to sit down and chat.

"How's school, honey?" Shayla's mother asked.

"It's amazing! It was tough adjusting at first and overcoming stereotypes, but I joined the basketball team and we're going to the nationals!" Shayla updated her.

"That's wonderful, honey! I'm so proud of you! We have to call your brother to inform him about the great news!" Her mother insisted.

"Austin! Guess what?" Mother hinted.

"What, Mom?" Austin replied.

"You sister is the team captain of her school's basketball team, and they're going to the national championships soon," Mother gladly updated him.

"Good work, sis, and good luck," Austin remarked.

"Thanks, bro," Shayla replied.

In essence, Shayla was overwhelmed by the happiness she was feeling, but she still had to work hard to win the next tournament and to shatter stereotypes.

A month later, the national championships commenced and it was time to give her absolute best to win.

The game started, and it was tougher than the previous match. The defense didn't allow them to pass the ball. And each time she managed to hold the ball, a member of the opponent's team snatched it from her.

The opponents were scoring easily because their defense had crumbled. They played like they had no hope of winning, yet they had come so far. Their outcome was worse than children in elementary school—there was no spirit or will; instead, it was like the opponents had sucked the life right out of them during the game.

During the break, they assembled in the locker room, eager to hear what Mr. Colby had to say. They needed words of encouragement so desperately. "We've come so far, and we can't give up now. Who thought we'd ever make it to the nationals? The truth is nobody yet here we are. We have to make this opportunity last! It means something to me and to all of us. It's our time to shine!" Mr. Colby encouraged ad then the other teammates repeatedly started chanting, "It's our time to shine!"

He'd just infused energy into them using uplifting word to break stereotypes. Their coach was brilliant.

As they went back to the court, they played like there was no tomorrow. The team's confidence was showing and sparked fear across the opponents. In turn, Shayla's team equalized the goals during the second half.

It was finally time to score the winning goal, yet time wasn't on their side. Shayla took it upon herself, dribbled the ball across the court, and scored the winning shot in the last second.

The audience roared with excitement. As she looked up, she could see my mother and brother who were cheering her on. Indeed, it was a wonderful day!

The winning team was rewarded with a trophy, and they celebrated the whole day. It was an unforgettable experience that eventually opened huge doors for Shayla in the future, making her one of the most prominent athletes in the U.S. She even broke barriers and height stereotypes by lovingly earning the cute nickname of "Sporty Shorty!"

Learned lessons

Even though you might be facing uncomfortable situations, you should remain positive and look for an opportunity to grow. Don't allow negative people to make you bitter. While many nicknames are cute and funny, bullying about height, weight, skin color, or body size is never acceptable, as Shayla's incredible story suggests.

Check out these fabulous extensions to practice the story's contents and related skills:

1. *Nickname Game: Recall Shayla's nickname and how it showed her ability to shatter stereotypes and to break barriers in basketball.*

2. *Basketball Ball: Imagine you're attending a basketball-themed dance, masquerade, or banquet. Sketch what you'll wear to this event. Be creative!*

3. *Name Frame: Jot down your given name as well as any nicknames you've acquired. Make a square frame around the one that feels the best and most uplifting to you.*

4. *Body Image: List 2-4 books, songs, or movies about body image and why we need to accept everyone exactly as they are.*

5. *N.C. Glee: Locate the state of North Carolina on an American map. Pin or mark where the Outer Banks area is.*

CHAPTER 5

A Field of Forgiveness, Confidence, and Problem Solving

*A*re you a fan of mysteries? Well, this story will keep you on your toes as it's action- packed, mature, and enthralling. This touching tale follows an awesome girl who has been living a huge lie throughout her entire young life.

As she pursues her track and field dreams in school, she encounters a big life secret that will make her a truth racer, as she faces how and why to choose self-belief over grief, stress, and doubt. She also masters the value of forgiveness, confidence, and problem solving skills. Will she eventually be able to fully believe in herself as she works hard to be the best track racer in America?

Travel today to a small town in Delaware, USA, to discover why self-belief matters and how to embrace it in your own life to meet your goals and to fulfil your dreams. It's also a great tale of family adversity.

It was a chilly morning in a small town called Tyler, Delaware. The cold and wet weather made the day seem a bit eerie—it was as if something unexpected would occur. My mother drove me to school, and I waited for class to begin. Immediately, the bell rang, and the new PE teacher entered the class with the principal.

"Good morning class, this is Miss Julia. She'll be your new substitute teacher." The principal, Mr. Martin, explained.

"It's nice to meet all of you, my name is Julia Montez, and I'll be your P.E teacher," she added.

I still couldn't wrap my head around it—*my previous P.E teacher was my track race coach, so how was I supposed to win the nationals now with this stranger?*

Everyone started murmuring, "Did you hear what happened to Mrs. Harrington?" Dalia, my best friend, whispered.

She didn't wait for my response and continued explaining, "She disappeared during her trip to Hawaii," she lamented.

"I didn't know!" I whispered.

Even though I wasn't fond of Mrs. Harrington and believed she was an oddball, I still felt terrible about the whole situation—no wonder she wasn't replying to my emails.

"Silence!" Mr. Martin commanded. The whole class was immediately so still that we all could hear a pin drop.

"Miss Julia was introducing herself until you rudely interrupted her," Mr. Martin added.

"It's fine, I'll take it from here," Miss Julia replied as she walked to the center of the class.

Mr. Martin strolled towards the door and disappeared through the corridors.

"Alright! It's time for P. E, I'll meet you in the field." We all went to the field and it was interesting. She was knowledgeable about track racing and so, I decided I'd ask her if she'd be willing to train me.

The bell rang, and it was time for recess. Before I went back to class, I decided to approach Miss Julia.

"Miss, can I have a moment?" asked politely.

"Why not?" She quickly responded. "What do you need?"

"I noticed you're very knowledgeable about track races. Mrs. Harrington was my previous coach, and I wanted to inquire if you'd train me since you're her substitute. I'll be heading to the nationals in two months," I explained.

"Of course!" She agreed with no hesitation, which was odd. I thought she'd say she had to think about it or simply decline the offer. What happened was highly unusual. Mrs. Harrington wasn't kind, but she was a good coach formerly. Miss Julia seemed nice from the first impression.

As I was walking home with my best friend, she began gossiping about Miss Julia.

"She just moved to our town. I heard she lost a child when she was young and never fully moved on with her life."

"What happened to the child?" I asked, sparking an interest, so she could talk more about it.

"Well, since she couldn't give birth because her womb was too delicate, the doctors suggested that she should let another woman carry a child for her," Dalia explained.

"Wait! Can someone else carry a child for you?" I asked. I was honestly shocked.

"Yes! It's a *thing* in the world of medicine. We're just too young to know about it, but we'll be taught one day," she said. "

"Alright, you can tell me more about Miss Julia's baby," I continued. I was shocked to hear how interested I was, yet I had just met the woman a few hours ago. She was nice to me, and so I felt terrible for her.

Nice people seem to go through so much difficult stuff, I thought.

"Well, once the other woman carried her baby for nine months, she ran away with the child once it was born, never to be found. Miss Julia is still looking for her missing baby who's now almost our age," Dalia explained.

"What a story! I hope Miss Julia finds her child. She seems like a good person," I replied.

"Yes, I agree," Dalia exclaimed..

"Where do you find all this *information* about teachers?" I asked.

"A true journalist never reveals her sources," she insisted.

"Alright! I understand, Miss Journalist." I replied.

That evening, we decided to rest at my place until the day ended and Dalia had to go back home. The following day was the weekend. I took my mother to the farmer's market. Surprisingly, we almost met Miss Julia, and my mother tried as much as possible to avoid her until we entered our car. I was shocked to see my mother act this way because of a teacher we barely knew.

"What's wrong, Mother?" I asked.

"Nothing! She just gave me a weird feeling and I had to leave," my mother murmured.

"I like Miss Julia; she's my P.E teacher, and she's really nice." I praised.

"I don't like her! Don't be too open or personal with her," my mother warned.

To make her less panicky, I agreed, but I still planned to attend race track and field practice. The weekend was fun, and I spent most of it with Dalia, but it ended pretty quickly, and it was time to go back to school.

As usual, Miss Julia was friendly and offered to train each day after school. We met at the field and she helped me practice daily.

Weeks passed, and I had grown fond of her. She showed me a new world to racing that I'd never seen before. She also believed in my dreams and motivated me to practice harder each day. After school, I went to her house, where it was warm and smelled of freshly baked tres leches cookies her mother had baked.

"Do you want one, *mija*?" The older woman offered.

"Thank you," I replied as I took a piece and popped it in my mouth.

The feeling I experienced while in Miss Julia's house was beautiful—it was truly as though I had known her and her mother for years. We all laughed and enjoyed the evening together. For the first time, I felt truly seen and understood. She also showed pictures of her participating in a track race when she was my age—she also had a massive collection of medals.

"Even when the world refuses to believe in you, you must always stay loyal to yourself and have faith in the possibility of achieving them," Miss Julia said as she put her collection of medals away. It was getting late, so I walked back home. When I arrived, I noticed that my mother tried to hide some papers, but I eventually found out they were plane tickets. We'd soon move out to another town.

"But why should we move somewhere else?" I asked. " All my friends live here! I also found a teacher I really like, and she's helping me with the track race. She believes in my dreams too,." I added, hoping my mother would understand me for the first time.

"I'm tired of this town; it's too crowded, that's all sweetie," she whispered as she hugged me, but I freed myself and ran upstairs.

How was I supposed to move to a new town, abandoning the possibility of achieving my dreams as one of the best track racers in America just because my mother felt it was too crowded? How could I explain this to Dalia? How could we move? The school year was just getting started! Everything felt off.

I couldn't sleep a wink that night. The following day, Mother explained we were moving the next day, so I had to bid my friends goodbye. The race was important to me because winning it would open a door of opportunities and the fact that my mother wanted me to throw away my dreams just because of her whims didn't sit right with me.

I was still not convinced—something weird was happening. Mom had been acting suspiciously since she saw Miss Julia.

At school, it was a frenzy of sorrow when I told my friends goodbye. Miss Julia was sad too—the evening we spent together with her mother was memorable.

"I wish you all the best, my girl," she cried as she hugged me. "I can drive you home," she offered, but I said no to the offer, knowing how my mother would react.

When I arrived home, there was a large truck outside, and two men were packing our furniture. I went to my room and packed everything. Suddenly, I had a knock on the door. It was Miss Julia.

She wanted to give me one of her medals—it was the first she'd ever won.

"This is to remind you that no matter where you go, always believe in yourself," she emphasized.

"Thank you," I replied.

After giving me the medal, she walked towards the door, but my mother entered and found her in our house. I knew I was in trouble since my mother didn't like Miss Julia.

"You! Where's my child?" Miss Julia started shouting, asking my mother for answers.

"I don't know what you're talking about," Mother replied as she ran towards me and hugged me tightly from the side.

"Is that my girl? Is it her? Why did you steal her from me?" Miss Julia asked; her voice was shaky yet powerful.

"I'm calling the police," she announced and dialled 911.

My brain knew what was happening, but I still couldn't wrap my head around it. I was still confused.

All this time, was I leaving with my kidnapper?

Police sirens could be heard from miles away. My 'mother,' or rather, the kidnapper, was still holding me tightly, so much so I couldn't breathe.

"Mom, let me go, you're hurting me," I tried to beg, but my pleas fell on deaf ears.

"Don't worry *mija,* the police will soon arrive," Miss Julia assured me.

Soon after, my kidnapper was arrested, and the court ruled that I was to stay with my biological mother, Maria Sanchez.

The next few days were tough—if my whole life was a lie how was I supposed to believe in anything? Even *myself.* Even though my real mother had found me, it felt like my whole world was crumbling down; and to top it all off, the national track race championships were in two weeks. *How was I supposed to move forward?* Nothing made sense and I fell into a depressive episode. I wouldn't wish it on my worst enemy.

"You can't run away from your problems, so you must face them to move forward," my grandmother insisted. So I decided to visit my other *mother* in prison to know why she did such an illegal act.

After having a long chat with her, it was clear that she was lonely and needed someone to love or to love her even at the expense of someone else. I chose to forgive her and the weight on my shoulders was lifted.

I went back home with a fresh perspective. Then I dedicated myself to building a truthful life for myself by believing in my abilities. Miss Julia, or rather my mother, helped me prepare for the championships. I used confidence and problem solving to become the track star I wanted to be!

Each morning, we'd woke up early and raced together. I was determined to win the race, so I added exercises that would increase my speed and strengthen my legs.

I wanted to succeed, and I believed I would.

Finally, the due date arrived and I woke up at the break of dawn for my morning run. Upon walking onto home, the aroma was enticing. My grandmother had prepared a delicious breakfast to make sure I was energized through the race. I was filled with so much love and it healed my heart.

At the race, most of my schoolmates attended to show their support, including my best friend. We lined up on the tracks and the race commenced. I had practiced for the 400-meter race, so I didn't have anything to worry about, I knew I could run fast.

It was a close race and my eyes were fixated on the finish line— I could see nothing else!

Even though my close opponent was proving to be tough to defeat, I won by a couple of seconds. While my victory wasn't expected by others since the competition was tough, I knew I'd cross the finish line first because I firmly believed in myself, used confidence, and applied problem solving skills.

The victory opened so many doors for me as I had anticipated. This was the beginning of my lifelong journey towards success, forgiveness, and peace!

Learned lessons

Again, as the story so dynamically displayed, we must emulate the main character/narrator in this story and forgive to life. We must be courageous and also problem solve effectively.

In other words, the challenges you face in life shouldn't weigh you down. They should motivate you to work hard for the life of your dreams because it's always at reach. Believe in yourself even when others don't. In a world full of lies, be the truth.

Now try your hand at these exciting post-reading challenges to incorporate the story's main ideas:

1. Quotable Quotes: Which quote or line from the story touches your heart and soul? Why? For me, I liked *"Nice people seem to go through so much difficult stuff,* I thought."

2. Delaware Dare: Go online with an adult's permission and locate 2-4 fun facts about this state. Glow with geography today!

3. Miss Julia: Write an "email" to Ms. Julia to thank her for the life lessons in the story. What would you say to her?

4. 2.0: If you were to create a movie, show, or cartoon based on this story, what would you call it and why?

5. Forgive to Live: Make a list of at least 5 people, personal ones, living, deceased, or even from history, that you want to forgive and explain why.

CHAPTER 6

Courage Amid the Climb: Tia Faces Fears And Banishes Tears

Tia, a young girl raised in a rural area in America's South, is extremely passionate about climbing in Tennessee's Smoky Mountains. However, she has one major problem to face: her paralyzing fear of heights, fear of failure, and fear that girls cannot excel in this sport.

On the other hand, her ultimate dream is to climb on top of the Swiss Alps in Europe. Yet she must face the difficulties on her path and *learn to be brave to achieve her dreams. Will she be able to face her fears, look beyond her them, and banish her tears?*

Start lacing up your hiking boots and find a sturdy walking stick because this story will take you on an educational and entertaining trek from North America to Europe. You'll climb to new heights in girl power, maturity, and socioemotional skills with talented Tia, a young mountaineer with lots of determination. She'll show that we can fizzle our fears by facing them directly with lots of confidence and courage!

Tia adored the blue sky in her home state of Tennessee, USA, ever since she was young. At age 3, she began climbing everything she could find, hoping to touch the azure sky, but she often couldn't climb down.

Her father Fernando, used to tell his wife, Elena, that Tia was heaven-sent, nicknaming her, "Angel." As Tia grew up, she realized that we can travel to the sky using planes, so her parents booked her first flight which made her realize that the sky was vast.

Her obsession with the sky ended shortly after the trip, but she still loved to climb and did it every chance she got, though it angered her cautious mother.

"Girl, get down!" Elena barked.

"Mama, I'm trying to save the crying kitty that's stuck on the tree,'" Tia insisted.

"Fernando! Fernando! She's climbing again!" Elena screamed in a shaky voice.

Her hidden terror was her daughter falling from the tree.

"Ah! My wife, you know she can't fall. Come here and stop worrying," Fernando asked, as she hugged his wife.

After getting a hold of the kitten, Tia carefully climbed down.

"You see, our daughter is a hero! We should be proud of her!" Fernando insisted.

"How can she mend her ways if you keep commending such appalling behavior from a young girl!" Elena disappointedly remarked as she left.

"She'll be alright," he assured, as he followed and tried to console her.

"Are you hungry?" Tia asked the kitty as she took it to the kitchen to feed it with milk.

"What did I say about bringing stray animals into the house? Tia, you never listen!" Elena argued.

"But Mama, I'm trying to feed the cat or it might die," Tia explained.

"Ah, my daughter, your heart is in the right place, but can you try to do things in a civilized way appropriate for girls?" Elena asked.

"Alright, Mama!" The young girl agreed and the two hugged.

"You'll squish the poor kitty, niña!" Elena warned.

"Oops! Sorry, kitty!" Tia whispered.

The family of three eventually had dinner and enjoyed a delicious meal.

"Papa, will you take me climbing on Saturday?" Tia begged.

"Why not! I sure will and we'll have a wonderful time, niña!" Fernando replied.

"You're always climbing! Why can't you find a *girly* sport like gymnastics? I'll even take you," Elena insisted.

"Mama, you know I love climbing! One day, I'll climb the biggest rock in Zermatt, Switzerland!" Tia cried.

At the climbing wall, the boys would whisper, "Oh dear! She's climbing!"

"Again?" Another would fret.

Tia was fascinated by climbing and even though she was short, she found a way to do it. Her courageous spirit always made her find a way!

After that fateful day, she decided to join the climbing team and told her parents. Her father was supportive but her mother hesitated.

Finally, the day she had been eagerly waiting for arrived. She was going to join the climbing team. She hopped out of bed and began preparing for the big day.

Since Tia was early during the try-outs, she went to the changing room to dress appropriately for the task.

She decided to warm up before try-outs by setting an amount of time to complete each boulder problem. Soon after, people started arriving and they could see her from above. They looked at her in disbelief, since they couldn't believe that a girl would actually be interested in climbing. Also, she seemed small, which put her at a disadvantage, but she was climbing perfectly fine.

Once everyone arrived, they lined up, waiting to be called.

"Phwwwwwhht!" The coach blew his whistle which let out a high-pitched sound, and once he had everyone's attention, he continued, "Thank you for coming! Today we'll be selecting the best climbers."

They sat on the floor, forming a circle, and began to introduce themselves.

Even though some of the boys wondered why Tia was there, that didn't bother her because she understood her goal—she was eager to make her dreams come true.

Once they knew each other, it was time for the try-outs. The boys showed off their tricks and it was finally Tia's turn.

She didn't stutter, as her confidence was unmatched. She courageously climbed the boulders, proving she'd end up being one of the best climbers. This was an important moment for her—she had to let go of her fear and show her skills, earning her a spot in the team.

As the days went by, she started making friends with the boys on the team who now respected her because she was a talented climber. She also started signing up for climbing competitions. Her dream was to go to Switzerland once she turned 18.

She was able to win most competitions, but she realized that since she was a girl, most opponents underestimated her and this was where she used to take advantage and end up victorious.

"Mama! Did you see? I've been winning competitions and I'm making some money," Tia revealed excitedly, but her mom's response proved that she was unhappy for her daughter. She even seemed disappointed.

"I'm happy for you, niña," Fernando acknowledged.

"Thank you Papa, I'll be able to travel to Switzerland very soon and you can accompany me!" Tia explained.

Fernando smiled and added, "You have two more years. Relax and enjoy the sport!"

Tia had big dreams for her future. As time went by, she won more medals and decided she wanted to attend a climbing program in Geneva, Switzerland to prepare for her trip.

Awhile back, she had seen try-outs for people who wanted to join the program. There was space for up to three people and every cost would be covered. She had the cut out of the article and taped it above her bed, so she applied the next day with the help of her dad.

One day after weeks of waiting, a letter arrived at the door. It was an invitation to join the climbing program in Geneva, Switzerland. She was beyond excited and couldn't contain her joy. This was a dream come true!

The next few days were full of frantic preparations. Deciding what to pack was proving to be more difficult than she had thought. She tried to bring as many essentials as possible but with some strategic help from her mother, she managed to pack everything she needed.

As she arrived at the airport, it started to hit her that she had to leave her family and she feared that she'd miss them terribly. Elena was there and even though she hadn't been supportive throughout, she was proud of Tia for being such a brave girl and fighting for what she believed in.

"This is an incredible opportunity," Elena said.

"I'm on my way to achieve my dreams; it feels so unreal!" Tia exclaimed.

"We're so proud of you," Fernando chimed in.

"You'll visit me soon, right?" She waved her parents goodbye, gathered all her stuff, and headed into the airport for her greatest adventure yet.

While waiting to board the airplane, Tia sat in disbelief. This was the first time she would travel alone to a new country that was miles away. Fear trickled down her spine, but she chose to be courageous.

Finally, it was time to board the plane. She remembered how much she used to adore the sky while she was a young niña and a teardrop fell on the ground. The step she was taking was one of the bravest things she'd ever done, so she bravely boarded and didn't look back.

The plane landed in Switzerland after a eight hours. As she arrived at the airport, she'd already fallen in love with the gorgeous country. Nature surrounded most parts of the city, allowing her to enjoy fresh air.

All her life she was used to indoor climbing walls, but this time, she was joining a program that would teach her how to rock climb, which was a scary experience but she chose to remain courageous.

Upon arrival at the institute, she was received warmly, even though the next few days were difficult to adjust. She called her parents as often as she could, but it wasn't the same.

She realized that rock climbing was more challenging than climbing boulders but that didn't stop her from trying harder to get the hang of it. After six months, the program ended and she decided to go to Zermatt where she would rock climb. She couldn't believe that she was finally going to achieve her dreams at a young age.

Tia didn't care about the world's recognition; she only wanted her own happiness, so this act of bravery gave her a sense of peace, even though she experienced a little anxiety.

The journey was beyond beautiful since she chose to ride on a train. She was able to admire Switzerland's splendor. After a few hours, she arrived at Zermatt and checked into her hotel. The next day was when she would go rock climbing to the Swiss Alps.

That night, she found it hard to sleep. While she was excited, she was also scared—but she chose to remain brave.

The next day, she woke up and prepared for the day. She carried all her essentials for the rock climbing retreat. They were accompanied by a guide and so the people who wanted to climb started climbing. It was definitely more difficult than what she was used to, but she knew this. Her goal was to ascend Matterhorn, which was a famous peak in the Swiss Alps.

The process wasn't easy, but her quick problem-solving skills allowed her to go higher as higher. Even when the people she started climbing with gave up and returned to the starting point, she kept pushing harder and chose to remain brave.

If she managed to climb the Swiss Alps, she'd be the youngest climber, at only 18 years old , to reach the peak of Matterhorn. With her determined spirit of never giving up, she was able to reach the top! She couldn't believe it. Her dream was now a reality!

After a few days, her parents came to visit her in Switzerland. When they saw her, they noticed a sparkle in her eye, like she was a new person who was happier and more alive.

Learned lessons

Like terrific, brave, and triumphant Tia displayed in this motivational tale, you shouldn't ever be afraid of making tough decisions in life kin order to achieve your targeted goals, outcomes, hopes, objectives, and dreams! Don't be fearful or timid. Approach life boldly like a lion.

Like the story's amazing protagonist, always try and choose to be brave because you never know where your courage could take you in life, friendship, or sports!

1. *Mountain Mama: Locate Switzerland on a European map and mark an X where the Swiss Alps are. Do they order other countries? If so, name them.*

2. *Problem Solving Power: Name 2-4 problems that you've recently faced like the main character in the book. How did you solve them? Which skills did you use?*

3. *Matterhorn Born: With an adult's permission, go online and research 2-4 fun facts about the Matterhorn. You may also check out a book about this topic from your local library.*

4. *It's a Climb: Draw a picture of a real mountain or a metaphorical one like trying out for cheerleader where you expressed courage and dedication. How did it feel to complete this challenge?*

5. *Courage Collage: Create a collage to demonstrate what courage means to you. Ask permission from grownups to use old newspapers, magazines, and other supplies.*

CHAPTER 7

No Horsing Around: Hadley's Social Activism and Justice for Animal Rights

Hadley wants to be a successful female equestrian, but she's tired of the abuse that many animals endure. Will she be the change the world of horse racing needs? At the same time, she also wants to become a future veterinarian, so can she balance both responsibilities?

She also has to overcome fears of not being good enough in both chosen paths, so read on to determine if she's able to.

If you're an animal lover, you'll adore this sweet tale with a tail! So stop horsing around and begin reading since it's packed with eminent life lessons about themes such as paying it forward, engaging in one's civic, ethical, and moral duties, and animal activism as far as social justice.

Beyond that, we'll gain geographical and cultural insights because this story takes place in rural Lexington, Kentucky, USA. Grab those cowgirl boots, a hat, and a saddle for a cool ride with Hadley!

The Lexington, Kentucky countryside lifestyle intrigued Hadley ever since she was a young girl. It had its charm that stood out to the young girl.

Unlike the noisy city center, it was quieter and the air was fresher. She enjoyed taking walks with her father; Robert, and they had fun adventures in the small town.

The pair had a spot on top of the hill where they would admire the whole region. The pepper-mint green vegetation spread across the land and the jewel-blue streams replenished the land, making it fertile.

The countryside was like paradise for Hadley and her father. Even though her mother didn't like visiting the area, she and her father would whenever he was free during the weekend.

Similarly, her father grew up in those natural lands and even though his childhood wasn't filled with luxury, he wanted to share the rural experience with his beloved daughter.

When Robert was just a boy, he dreamt of being a jockey, so he was well-versed in the sport and taught his daughter from a young age. He wasn't teaching her because he wanted her to become a famous jockey, he only did it because he yearned to connect with his daughter using a sport he used to play at a young age.

However, his career was cut short because his family wasn't rich and at the time Equestrians typically came from rich families, but his parents simply couldn't afford it. Now and over the years he worked hard to provide his daughter what he lacked as a young boy and bought a ranch where he filled the stables with different animals.

Robert would accompany Hadley to their ranch where they'd go to the stables to spend time with the horses. He'd put her on a horse with him and the pair would trot on the horse for hours.

When she was old enough, her father would put Hadley on a horse, letting her walk it while he guided her on the side. At first, the thought of riding the horse alone scared the young girl, but she was brave just like her father. Then within no time, she was able to ride alone.

When she was 16, she decided that her love for horses wasn't just a hobby; instead, she wanted to take the sport seriously because she was passionate about horse races. During the weekends, if she wasn't at the ranch with her father, she was at the horse stables in Lexington.

She had mastered a special way to connect with animals and her friends had nicknamed her, "the animal whisperer." Whenever an animal was having trouble, she was able to determine the issue and relieve it. Even though she was passionate about derbies, she was appalled about the treatment that horses were often subjected to and fought against their abuse. She knew that horses had to be ridden correctly so they wouldn't suffer from any health problems and decided to teach riding at the local racing training course.

"You have the potential to be an excellent vet!" Her students and the people who watched her cater to animals encouraged.

It was at the back of her mind, but she wanted to start focusing on her equestrian career. At such a young age, she had big aspirations and her father was her biggest influence. Even though she came from a wealthy family, she still had good moral values.

"Papa, I've decided. I want to take horse racing seriously. I want to be a jockey," Hadley revealed on a memorable night.

"Honey, I don't think your mother would approve," Robert warned.

"It's what I want. It's my dream and you taught me to fight for what I want in life," she replied.

"Fair enough! I'll talk to your mother and give you a response!" He remarked.

"Thanks, Pa!" Hadley grinned.

That night, she had a vivid dream that she couldn't wrap her head around. She dreamt that she had two horses that were racing and both won the race at the same time.

But, isn't one horse supposed to win, not two? She wondered.

She woke up and went downstairs for breakfast where she found her mother enjoying the meal.

"Your father tells me you want to be an equestrian, so he wants to hire a coach for you," Her mother said.

"Really?" Hadley said excitedly.

"I'm still thinking about it. Hold your horses! No pun intended," Her mother replied.

Hadley chuckled and exclaimed, "I know you'll support me, Mama. I want to ask you something about a dream I had last night."

Her mother had a strong intuition and was able to see things in a clear perspective. In turn, she told her mother the dream.

"I think it means you'll pursue two different fields and be successful at both!" She replied. "I have to go to work, I'll tell you what I think about horse racing tonight," she added while she gave Hadley a kiss on the forehead.

Since it was a school day, Hadley went to school and it ended pretty fast. Then she went straight home. She was hoping her mother would say yes to her suggestion since it was what she wanted to do with her life. Specifically, she also wanted me to feel the bliss she experienced while riding a horse forever: and being a jockey was the only way to do that.

During dinner, her parents were present.

"What have you decided?" Hadley inquired.

"You'll start training next week," her mother responded.

Hadley was so pleased with the happy news and couldn't contain her excitement. This was the beginning of her journey to being a professional jockey. As she went to sleep that night, she couldn't help but wonder what would happen during her first training session. Her excitement was slowly turning into fear—*fear of not being good enough.*

It was an odd feeling, since she'd been praised all her life for her amazing skills. She even taught horseback riding at the country club. But, it was different. *Teaching and competing to win were two different things.*

The following day she woke up early to prepare for the session with her trainer, Paloma. Hadley showered and sat on the bed in her towel, a little bit scared. Well, it was her first training session and was completely normal for her to feel a little bit frightened. In addition, she was a perfectionist who never gave herself enough time to grow. In her mind it was either she was good during the first trial or she sucked.

She wanted to shine during the first session and this increased her anxiety. Next, footsteps approached and there was a knock on the door. She got up and answered it.

"What's wrong, honey? I thought you'd be excited for your first training session," Hadley's mom inquired.

"I'm just a little bit," Hadley hesitated.

"Scared?" Her mom asked.

"Yes..what if I'm not cut out for competitions? What if I'm only good enough at teaching? What if.." She hesitated again.

"Hadley, you can trust me, I promise this is a safe space for you to speak about your feelings," her mom encouraged.

"What if I'm not good enough?" Hadley questioned while she shied away.

"I believe in you and you're good enough. Sweetie, everything you want to achieve today is possible; the day has just begun. Now all you need to do is to believe in yourself as well and you'll be alright!" Hadley's mom expressed while giving her a warm hug. She became more confident and her mother helped her get ready.

"Remember, you're a teacher and young children look up to you. This isn't something new, you just need to adjust to compete. You've got this!" Her mom added.

Hadley wore her silks, hat, and boots and went downstairs to eat her breakfast.

"I prepared to give you energy throughout the day, you'll do great!" Her father said as he flipped a pancake. Hadley sat at the dining table and enjoyed her meal.

"Thanks, Daddy!' She voiced.

Dad drove her to the Country Club for her first training session. On the way, he told her about how he also wanted to be a jockey when he grew up too, his situation at home at the time didn't allow him to pursue the career. Hadley was shocked to hear about it. During the times they went on adventures together, he never spoke about it. This made her connect with her father more.

Now more than ever, she knew that she was destined to be a jockey. So during the training practice with Miss Paloma, Hadley was able to prove that she was a skilled equestrian.

As months passed by, her skills improved and Miss Paloma started signing her up for local competitions. Hadley won most of the time, thus pushing her to the top jockey's list. Even though she was the last on the list, it was still a great accomplishment. The list contained numerous men, but there were only three female jockeys.

At this point in her life, she started realizing that her accomplishments weren't just her own, as she shared them with other girls. If she won, they would be winning as well, so she completed the work and soon moved to top 10.

As she practiced tirelessly to be the best jockey in the country, she also took it upon herself to take care of the animals in the nearby stables. Her love for them allowed her to find unique solutions to assist them.

"You should consider being a vet!" One of the stable hands suggested.

"I've heard it before too many times and perhaps you're right," Hadley replied.

She decided to sign up for veterinary school to join while in college.

"I've decided to be a Vet as well," she broke the silence as she was having dinner with her parents.

"That's good news, but are you sure you'll be able to manage being an equestrian and veterinarian? It seems like it's too much responsibility. You're still young and you have lots of time," her mother added.

"Mom, do you remember the dream?" Hadley asked.

"What dream?" Robert asked.

"I dreamt that two of my horses won a competition. I feel like I'm destined for this," she confirmed.

After hearing this, her parents gave her the support she needed.

Months later, she moved from ninth position to second. Miss Paloma was happy and wanted her to claim the first position, so she signed Hadley up for the national equestrian championships. If she won the title, she'd be the youngest and first woman to do so.

The following days were filled with many riding lessons. For example, they focused on speed and sturdiness. Hadley also targeted schoolwork because she wanted her GPA to be high enough for Harvard School of Veterinary Science.

At first, it was hard balancing both responsibilities especially since she was preparing for the final battle, but as time went by, she got the hang of it and flourished in her final exams with a high GPA. She was also spoiled for choice because she was called by a variety of elite universities.

Then finally, it was time for the equestrian championship and she was competing against a top jockey who had never lost a race before. Her parents were there to support her and boost her confidence.

Before the race started, Hadley made it clear that she didn't want to hit the horse as she raced. She was certain that her connection with the horse was enough. This shocked the masses and spread awareness on animal cruelty in horse racing.

Many disapproved, but she knew she could do it—she was confident and believed in the horse she picked.

The race began and the two began competing. In the beginning, it was clear that her opponent was in control because she beat the horse, making it run faster, but Hadley was much gentler with the horse. Finally, to everyone's surprise, she started getting ahead and approached the finish line.

All at once, Hadley's horse jumped across the finish line. While the opponent had been formerly ahead, this move sealed Hadley's victory, giving her the top spot.

In brief, her parents were also so proud of her active contribution to animal welfare, ethics, morals, social justice, and activism.

Learned lessons

You don't have to do things just because you found them that way. You can change the world with new ideas. You can be a pioneer, an innovator, or whatever you like.

As Hadley so effectively modelled in this superb story, we must never be scared to be yourself, follow our dreams and heart, affirm that we're all indeed good enough. By fizzling fears, we can step into our confidence and power. We can also purge perfectionism and realize that we're all perfectly imperfect, and we can learn from mistakes and grow from flaws.

Lastly, engage in some extra activities to explore themes from the story:

1. Flex in Lexington: Find Lexington, Kentucky on a U.S. map. What rivers, highways, landmarks, and other prominent features do you notice? Which cities are also within driving distance of it?

2. Derby Drama: With your parents' permission, go online and research the history of the Kentucky Derby or another other famous ones you can find. Jot down 2-4 fun facts.

3. Purging Perfectionism: Make a list of skills or areas in your life where you tend to be a perfectionist. Set a goal to make it less stressful and more realistic for you in these areas and skills to purge that sense of perfectionism and embrace that we're all perfectly imperfect!

4. Mirror, Mirror: In order to confirm that you're good enough, make up a positive affirmation and read it 10 times in front of a mirror to encourage yourself.

5. Jazzy Jockey: Identify the top 3 skills that a jockey should possess.

CHAPTER 8

Gabby's Golden Goal: A Clear Mind Equals Success Divine

Are you a fan of the exciting game of softball? Whether you're on a grass field or in an indoor stadium, this sport offers great exercise and challenge. Along the same lines, this incredible story follows a Gabby, a determined, focused, resilient, young softball player who has to deal with her sick mother while trying to excel as one of the world's top players in the sport.

Highly goal-oriented and very motivation, Gabby hits balls and catches in her sport with power and precision but also her golden goals with perseverance and a competitive mindset. Her hometown of San Diego, California serves as the tale's setting as well as a visit later to Oceania in Sydney, Australia.

Jump for joy and aim for a homerun with Gabby now as we discover how a clear and focused mindset leads us to success divine. In other words, when we set our minds on an outcome or goal, we can pursue it with lots of optimism.

Gabby grew fond of softball ever since her mother bought her a bat. Later on, she participated in inter-school championships throughout her school life and her team won the most games.

She soon blossomed into a beautiful young woman and her achievements were starting to pay off. During one of her high school games, a coach took an interest in her and offered to serve as her agent and coach. Mr. Dennis was fascinated by the girl's skills and believed with proper practice, she'd end up being one of the best softball players in the world.

So the pair practiced as often as they could and within a short time, she had moved from being the 6th best player in the US to second. The national team sought her out after this occurrence and she'd soon represent the country in the worldwide championships in Sydney, Australia!

The opportunity was once in a lifetime and so her agent urged her to accept it as soon as possible. The first team meeting was enjoyable, unlike the girls from high school. Here they were more poised and friendlier. Everyone took it upon herself to find ways to elevate the team. The whole experience was nothing short of amazing.

As the years passed by, Gabby's mother's mental health deteriorated since the passing of her father. They had to admit her in a mental institution, which saddened Gabby, but she had to work hard to afford treatment that would heal her mom.

The worldwide championships were soon approaching and she had to fully commit to the games. Regardless of what she was going through, she had to focus on the present moment in order to yield success divine.

The following day she had to meet Mr. Dennis who would later tell her all about the trip to Sydney as he had discussed with the U.S. members of the softball association.

Since Mr. Dennis knew the sea calmed Gabby immensely, he decided to meet her where they'd enjoy the waves as they crashed.

It was a beautiful summer day in Butterfly beach, California. The sun shone brightly, making the water in the sea glitter. Gabby sat on a sea rock and wrote a letter to her pen pal, Dina, letting her know that Gabby would be visiting Sydney soon.

Dear Dina

My coach and I will be visiting Sydney soon. I can't wait to meet you!

Love,

Gabby

"What are you writing?" Mr. Dennis inquired. "I just want to visit my friend while I'm in Sydney. They have a farm and we can enjoy a weekend there!" She explained.

"That's a good idea but you have to focus on the team and practice harder than before. The games are in a week," Mr. Dennis remarked.

"What else?" Gabby asked.

"I have your first paycheck, and two tickets to Sydney. We'll leave next week Friday." Mr. Dennis voiced. But tomorrow, don't be late for practice," he warned.

"Alright!" Gabby replied.

Once Mr. Dennis left, Gabby jumped into the sea. The ocean lifted her up and she floated while looking at the sky. At this moment, nothing else mattered and she felt as though her problems were melting into the deep blue sky.

Later that evening, she folded the letter and placed it in an envelope.

The next day, she gave Tom the postman the letter.

"Hey! Who's the letter for and where's it going?" Jerry the postal worker asked.

"Hey Tom!" The two bumped their fists together.

"It's for my friend, Dina! She lives in Sydney, Australia." Gabby added.

"Alright then! It'll arrive sooner than you think!" Tom promised as he waved and walked away.

"Thank you, Tom." Gabby exclaimed as she waved back and walked into the house.

Gabby was excited to visit Sydney, since she had been friends with Dina for two years, and finally, they'd meet.

She was also able to pay the medical bills using the check she'd received and still had some leftover money to use.

The following day she arrived at softball practice earlier than everyone and began to train on her own. On that particular day, she focused on improving her speed but also on running on the track a few times. Her teammates arrived and they all practiced together. It was a great experience for everyone since each person understood their responsibilities and wanted to win the championship games.

Days passed by swiftly, and it was time to travel to Sydney.

"Gabby? Did you pack everything you need?" Mr. Dennis, who understood the amount of pressure she was subjected to, came to help her prepare for the trip.

"Yes! I'm ready!" She replied as she walked down the stairs with her backpack.

"You're carrying a backpack?" Mr. Dennis asked in disbelief, "Will it fit everything you need?"

"I added all the essentials. I just need the softball bat my mother bought for me," Gabby replied.

"It wasn't my intention to trigger you," Mr. Dennis remarked.

Gabby smirked, showing that she didn't take it to heart.

The duo took a cab to the airport. As they arrived, she still couldn't believe that her dreams were finally coming true, but neither of her parents were there to witness it, which made her sad.

"Enough sadness, you must enjoy this moment. You've earned it," Mr. Dennis commended. Not only was he her coach and agent, he was also becoming her friend.

Gabby video called Dina as they wait to board the plane.

"Hey! Did you receive my letter? I can't wait to meet you! I must say I rarely have time to make new friends, but your letters have helped me so much!" Gabby explained.

"Yes, I did and I can't wait to meet you too! Your letters have been good for me too! Will you come to our farm for a tour? My father is hosting a farmer's market where all farmers can sell fresh produce to the public," Dina asked.

"Yes! I'd love to visit your farm. As soon as I land, we'll definitely plan something. I'll be participating in the softball championship so you can come and watch me. Talk to you soon, since our plane is ready to take off," Gabby explained as she ended the video call.

Gabby and Mr. Dennis walks towards the plane; the duo located their seat, and immediately after, the plane departed. Gabby sat by the window to admire the view. She re-read Dina's letters because they both went through similar occurrences.

They were introduced to each other by a therapist since they both wanted to find someone who would understand their situation, but the only condition was that person was supposed to be living miles away. Both of their mothers developed mental disorders and had to be checked in a hospital. They started writing letters anonymously, then they introduced each other virtually, and now they were going to meet.

After a couple of hours, Gabby and Dennis arrived in the colorful city of Sydney.

The skyscrapers stretched, almost touching the sky. Australia was quite similar to the U,S., but the climate was different. She was also thrilled to know that where they'd be staying had a beach nearby.

They were to rest the next day since the whole team was jet lagged, so they decided to visit the farm. Gabby contacted Dina to inform her about her arrival, who was so pleased and ended up welcoming her to her father's farm the next day for the farmer's market.

That night, Gabby couldn't sleep. Being in a new country caused anxiety, so she decided to call Dina. "You should have confidence that things will fall in place and let go of so much fear!" Dina explained and her words calmed Gabby, who was able to sleep peacefully.

The next day, the sun rose, casting golden rays through Gabby 's window.

She woke up and prepared for the farm visit. As she went downstairs to eat breakfast. Mr. Dennis was waiting for her while he was sipping a cup of tea.

"Will you accompany me?" She asked.

"Of course," he said as he sipped his tea.

She ate her breakfast and then she and her coach entered a vehicle that took them to the farm.

"Isn't a farm supposed to be in the countryside, not the city center?" Mr. Dennis broke the silence.

"It's rather weird, right? That's why I want to see it!" Gabby said as she chuckled.

After a few hours, they arrived at the farm which was on the outskirts of Sydney.

The area was filled with green vegetation and farms that stretched through miles and miles away.

"It's beautiful, isn't it?" Gabby said as she admired.

"Mmm hh mm!" Mr. Dennis agreed.

As they arrived at the farm, Dina and her father gave them a warm welcome.

"It's a pleasure to finally meet you," Dina remarked as she gave Gabby a hug.

"Dad, this is Gabby. She's my pen pal turned *real pal* from California," Dina explained.

"I'm Martin! It's so good to finally meet you! I hear you're representing your country in the softball competition," Mr. Martin commented as he gave them all a farm tour.

"Yes! It's such a big responsibility, but with a great agent and coach on my side, it's easy to manage," she replied.

"No. You're the one who's easy to manage because you're so talented!" Mr. Martin insisted.

"Your business partnership is a match made in Heaven!" Dina praised.

They began the tour at the strawberry farm, which was beautiful! Gabby had never seen anything like it. The farmers were also treated fairly and with respect. The strawberries sat upon the grass, filling the farm with a sweet smell.

Next, Dina explained that every worker on their farm was important and treated with respect because their hard work was why their farm was doing so well.

The farmers gave them a few berries to taste. Gabby had never eaten such sweet strawberries before. "The strawberries are sweet because they're grown with love and care. The secret is love," Drew maintained.

"Mmhh! So yummy! Love is truly a good secret potion," Gabby chuckled. By this time, Mr. Dennis and Martin had already diverted to another area and the pair enjoyed their time together.

The whole experience brought a sense of peace in Gabby's heart. And once the day ended, she invited them to her game that would be held in two days.

Gabby and Mr. Dennis went back to their separate hotel rooms early because she had practiced the next day.

That night she was able to sleep peacefully once again. Australia was giving her the peace she had always yearned for; and instead of feeling powerless about her mother's situation, she decided when she went back home, she'd appreciate the fact that her mother was still alive, even though she was unwell.

The following day she met up with the girls and practice was smooth as usual.

Finally, the day of the tournament arrived and it was time to show what she was made of. Drew and her father arrived to show their support and they sat with Mr. Dennis. The time of the game was getting closer and Gabby grew more nervous by the minute.

The national teams of both countries; America and Australia assembled in the field, ready to fight for the championship game. The field was shaped like a diamond and the audience cheered with excitement.

When the game started, Gabby carefully observed the rival team's pitcher preparing. Since she was this chosen pitcher, it was her job to do absolutely anything to get on base. At this moment, she breathed heavily and as she held onto the bat, she noticed she wasn't clutching it as firmly as she should've.

Gabby started to take heavy breaths and remembered what her mother used to say, "Be confident in whatever you do." She then took a perfect swing and the pitcher of the rival team began to run. Gabby also raced to get to the next base and they scored a point.

In turn, her teammates screamed with excitement and after the first goal, the rest came easy as they won. She eventually dedicated the victory to her mother.

Learned lessons

No matter how hard the goal is or the dream's level of difficulty is, Gabby's tale taught us that you should always remain confident, clear in your mindset, and be courageous. As long as you believe in yourself, you can achieve anything you want like Gabby did in her young life.

After traveling from San Diego, California, USA to Sydney Australia, now you can practice further from your own home or room as you engage in these free exercises:

1. Sydney Virtual Tour: Go Down Under to Australia today. Find a top tourist attraction in Sydney and locate 2-4 fun facts about this amazing destination.

2. Softball Swag: Draw a softball on paper. Then fill it in with softball related words, famous players, equipment, etc. Aim for 2-4 labels.

3. Clear Mind: Jot down 2-4 ways you can improve your focus and clear your own mind in life, school, sports, etc.

4. Gabby's BFF: Imagine you're Gabby's best friend. Pretend to make a dialogue between them about where Gabby will be in 10 years from now.

5. San Diego Trip: Create a five-day itinerary for you and your family to visit San Diego. What will you see, eat, and do? Where will you stay? Conduct some fun research.

CHAPTER 9

Lily's Row and Glow: Teamwork Makes the Dream Work!

L*ily is passionate about rowing, but she still has a lot to learn. Will she face all the difficulties thrown her way in life to achieve her dreams despite trying the sport later on in her life? Can she also defy the odds and learn to embrace the power of teamwork? Will she acquire vital leadership skills along the way in this senSEAtional story?*

Lily's face would light up every time her father would let her go fishing with him.

In retrospect, her journey to being one of the most renowned rowers began when she was just six years old. She lived with her father in a small fishing town in The Florida Keys that had little to no rowing experts. She learned how to row on the ocean with her father during his fishing expeditions.

While her father worked tirelessly to provide food on the table by selling fish, she accompanied him from time to time to learn all about the sea and occasionally went rowing using her father's small boat. As a result, all these experiences shaped her life because she eventually got a scholarship to study Marine Biology in Yale. Still, her dream of being a rower was embedded in her mind.

There was a national water sports center nearby, known as Holme Pierrepont, where she'd go to watch rowing events.

Since she wanted to actively make changes that would allow her to become a rower, she hatched a plan to join one of the competitions even though she had little experience. All she had was passion and knowledge of the sea and even though she knew how to row, she soon realized that the rowing she was used to was different compared to the one in the competitions.

The following day, Lily woke up at the break of dawn and prepared to go to her classes which ended during the afternoon. Afterwards, she went to the water sports center to apply for the competition.

"Do you have any teammates?" The woman who was signing up the competitors asked.

"No, is it necessary?" Lily naively asked.

The woman didn't take her seriously and called the next group to sign up. She honestly didn't know where she'd find eight rowers who'd agree to compete with her.

She was disappointed and went back to her hostel. As she was climbing up the stairs, something peculiar occurred.

"We need an eighth member for the rowing competition! Mikey just cancelled because he's sick," the voice explained. Lily hurriedly went back downstairs and offered herself as a substitute.

"How can we be certain you're a good rower?" The girl asked.

"You can audition me!" Lily offered.

"Alright! I work at the national water sports center, we can go right now," the girl suggested.

"Cool!" Lily agreed.

The pair went to the water sports center and Lily got in the rowing boat, as the girl entered as well and the two began to row together.

"Hmm, not bad! You're in, I'm Zoe by the way!" The girl greeted.

Lily couldn't believe her ears, and she was happy because it was the start of something bigger in her life.

"I'm Lily! I'll be happy to join the team," she said.

"Don't get too excited though, because you'll only be the substitute," Zoe warned.

"Still good enough for me," Lily replied as she walked away.

"We meet tomorrow at 6pm for practice. The competition is in two days!" Zoe voiced.

"Got it!" Lili added.

The following day Lily went to classes as usual and later on, she went to practice rowing with the crew. They were all friendly and understood the importance of teamwork—except Zoe who was hard to work with.

Then the day of the competition arrived and they all assembled at the center to take part in it. After a lot of practice, they were able to win. Lily was also a valuable addition and helped the team win because she had strong hands that allowed her to row faster than the rest.

They all agreed to make her a permanent member and the crew signed up for more competitions throughout Yale and sometimes they won and other times, they lost but that didn't stop them from trying again and again.

All of them wanted to take part in the worldwide rowing competition that would be held in Bali, Indonesia. Unlike rowing on the lakes as they were used to, they'd row on a sea that had waves so they knew they had to practice harder with each passing day.

After a few years, the whole crew's skills grew tremendously and they were chosen to take part in the competition in Bali.

The following day they flew to Bali. The journey took a couple of hours but they arrived safe and should.

As they arrived, they were in awe at the beauty Bali offered. Lily was glad that it was near the sea. In a few days, they'd be taking part in the worldwide competition and this made her happy.

The day of the competition arrived and all the rowers began competing for the long-distance championship. The sea was calm and they were making progress until the sun fell away and the weather changed. Thunder cracked loudly, giving a warning that a storm was approaching.

"We have to go back!" A scared Zoe insisted.

"No, we need to keep going forward," one of the rowers instructed.

"We've come a long way to quit," Lily encouraged, so they decided to keep rowing.

Rain started pouring down and other teams decided to go back to the shore, except Lily's team.

After hours of rowing, they realized it would be a rough passage back to the shore because of the rain just pouring down until nightfall. The night was cold, dark clouds covered the moon, strong winds blew across the sea, the waves crashed against the rowing boat which was practically small, causing it to sway sideways.

With each passing minute, the crew grew wearier because they realized they were lost. As they rowed across the angry sea, they found a small island.

"We should row to seek refuge on the Island," Zoe instructed. "I told you we should go back. to the shore but you wouldn't listen," She added.

"What do you say, Lily?" One of the teammates asked.

"Why are you asking her? She's the one who agreed to this!" An angry Zoe argued.

All at once, Lily could feel a wave of confusion overpowering her. She had to make a decision and she had to make it fast, so that her crew could survive the tempest.

"Prepare to row towards the Island," Lily advised.

"Aye aye, Captain!" One of the Rowers replied as he did as he was told.

The night wasn't pleasant and most rowers were uneasy. They were scared of their new path and what it would bring. In a final blow, a mountainous wave split the boat in two and one side of the boat fell into the sea, sinking deep into the unknown.

The rowers jumped into the sea and swam to the shore across the sea. They had lost everything that could've led them back home. The island they found themselves in was dark and no vegetation grew.

How would they survive? What food would they eat?

Fear and many questions raced through their minds.

"It's all your fault. If only you listened to me!" Zoe confronted Lily.

"Oh really? We came here to win this competition. How was I to know a storm would approach? This is nobody's fault and if we want to find a way back home, we need to stick together. If you're with me, follow me to find food, and tomorrow we will come up with a way to get back home. If you're not, you can stay here. It's your choice." Lily offered as she walked away.

Since she had studied Marine biology, it came in handy since she was able to find places where fish would be in the sea. Also, her knowledge of fishing allowed her to find food for the crew.

The night was cold and foggy. They lit a fire but the cold winds were too strong. It was the worst night of most of the rowers. All they wanted was to go home, back to their families.

The sun rose the next morning and shone brightly, casting golden rays on Lily's face, waking her up for another day full of hardship.

Lily woke up her crew and they all toured the island. During the day, the island wasn't as bad as the night. It was warm and adventurous. During the night it was cold and empty. They also realized that the Island was far from civilization. They had to find a way to survive.

"I'll try to build a boat, so it can take us home," Lily said.

"Do you believe her? She's the cause of all of these issues," Zoe warned.

The following days were filled with anguish, they didn't have clean water to drink so they decided set out to discover more about the island and hopefully they'd find a stream

The next day they all went to look for food and water and as they approached the other side of the island, they saw a small stream. The water was fresh and not salty, so they gladly drank it.

As Lily gazed into the water, she saw something glistening so she decided to take it out. It was an axe and she took it out. She would then use it to make a boat so the whole crew could row to safety.

The crew decided to stick with Lily's leadership during the hard time to make it a bit easier—except Zoe, who was getting weaker with each passing day. They even used the sharp knife to cut through trees to make a wooden boat and oars.

Since the island had a few resources the process was slow, but they all hoped another ship would approach, and they'd all board and leave to safety and have access to basic needs.

Yet that didn't happen, as the hours became days, and the days became months.

Through each passing day, the crew grew weary and tired.

The rocky island was hard to survive in because of the scorching sun during the day. But—at least Lily's knowledge of plants and medicine allowed them to find food and medicine.

The other crew members weren't angry at Lily, though, because they all decided they wanted to row. Zoe was angry because they wouldn't listen to her and so she apologized to her and they all decided to stick together as a team.

By working together, they were able to finish the boat in a few weeks. Finally, they would bid the island goodbye. The due date to return home arrived and they all got in the boat, hoping it'd be strong enough to take them back home.

The wooden boat wasn't sturdy or fast so they had to paddle as fast as possible and to top it all off, they were lost at sea and couldn't figure out a way to find the shore they were in during the competition.

The more they paddled, the more they felt lost. It was as if they were going around in circles until Lily looked at the signs of dry land nearby and pointed them in the right direction.

As they approached the shore, there were policemen and people gathered around—it was a search party that had lasted months.

"It's them!" One of the people at the shore screamed as soon as she saw us and the sea police drove their catamaran towards us, taking them to the shore.

Even though the competition hadn't gone as planned, they still used their rowing skills to save themselves, earning them a special trophy. Lily reunited with her father and the two travelled the world by sea together.

Until today, Lily is still seen as one of the best rowers in the world by leading her team out of danger through teamwork.

Learned lessons

No matter how challenging life becomes, you have to keep going. And when you make mistakes, acknowledge them quickly so you can rectify your life and make it better. Use all your experiences to learn.

Glow and grow with teamwork and leadership, like Lily firmly exhibited in this action-packed story.

Try rowing with these fun, interactive post-reading exercises to extend your knowledge and creativity.

1. Bali Blitz: Locate Bali on a map or a world atlas. Notice its major cities, which geographical features, etc. Which continent is it located on?

2. Leadership Limerick: Create a short poem, rap, song, or rhyme about the power of leadership.

3. Setting Smiles: Where does the story first take place in America? Which state?

4. Teamwork: Reflect on a successful experience that you've had when you worked well on a time. What happened? In contrast, name an experience you had that was unsuccessful. How could teamwork have enriched your outcomes?

5. Row and Grow: With an adult's permission, research 2-4 fun facts about this sport, its history, where it's the most popular, etc.

CHAPTER 10

Neva Breaks The Ice in Skating: Conquering Life One Step at a Time!

This is a touching story about a young girl named Neva who lives in Omaha, Nebraska, USA. She dreams of eventually becoming a successful figure skater. Will she choose the path her father planned for her or will she learn to make her own destiny?

In brief, this heart-warming story suggests that we all have the power in the NOW. When we stay rooted in the present moment and *mindfully focus on what want, our strengths, and our goals, we can fully immerse in the here and now. Plus, we can further engage with our senses and learn to embrace an attitude of gratitude, like Neva in this tale eventually masters.*

Are you eager to break the ice and get yourself a true gift of gratitude? Think of gratitude like a crown or a sparkling tiara and get some bling to zing today!

In a cheerful town called Omaha, Nebraska, USA, where the days were chilly but the skies blue, there lived a special girl called Neva. She was the kindest kid in her heartland neighborhood. Everyone admired how caring she was—if anyone was in trouble, she always tried her best to solve the problem.

Since she was as smart as a fox, she was able to create unique solutions, gaining the admiration of the people in her community at a young age. Yet her biggest dream was to become a professional figure skater, so she spent hours learning the sport. What made Neva stand out to the rest was her graceful and grateful presence— when she was on the blanket on cold ice, you could feel it.

Her father; George, was a doctor. He cured a lot of people in the village. All his patients praised him since he was good at his job. Also, like his daughter—he was a kind man, but he wanted Neva to follow a similar path and become a doctor.

Furthermore, he knew that her selfless personality would allow her to become a great doctor.

Her mother was a nurse but died shortly after she was infected with an unknown disease. This pushed Neva's father to learn more about medicine to find a cure for the rarest diseases.

At first, Neva decided to follow her own path. She was a talented figure skater who yearned to hear the audience's applause after performing. Her dream was to play both characters in Swan Lake at the same time, which was difficult because the art form was mainly done in ballet not, in figure skating. Yet her willingness to learn and determination to succeed made her practice harder with each passing day.

Plus, she was also a creative and a grateful soul and was able to curate new moves that she'd show her friends at school and they'd cheer.

Naturally, Neva started her journey towards becoming a figure skater at a young age. She practiced often at the Ice skating arena but her father wasn't supportive of her dream. "You should accompany me to the hospital," George hinted.

"I have skating practice," Neva replied.

As Neva grew, she exceled more at figure skating. Even when she was young, her wonderful work was admired by all around her. Her talent shone brighter with each passing day. She always showed compassion and gratitude.

But no matter how hardworking she was, Neva was still a dreamer at heart. She remembered how her mother once said, "If you want your dreams to come true, whisper your wishes to the stars and their light will lead the way!"

So every night, she'd sit outside and stare at the stars. Every so often, she'd hope the stars would grant her wish. "I yearn to become the best figure skater in the whole region," she politely requested. "I'd really love to watch the audience's applause," she added.

After saying this, the largest star in the group of stars twinkled brightly. Then upon practicing at the skating arena, she went straight back home. To keep her mother's dream alive; every night she'd sit at her window, admiring the stars and politely whisper, "I wish to become the best figure skater in the whole country."

The largest star twinkled once again. Slowly by slowly, it became a habit, and every single night, Neva went to see the stars to ask them to grant her wish after her every dance practice.

Years passed, and she blossomed into a beautiful young woman but still, every night, she asked the stars to grant her wish. All she wanted was to manifest her purpose and align her destiny with the Universe.

Besides, Neva was a smart girl, so she graduated high school and went to an Ice skating school in New York, where she bumped shoulders with some of the most talented artists and world's greatest Olympians.

"Your dream is to play both characters in Swan Lake at the same time as a figure skater?" People often asked in shock.

"Yes," she'd gladly admit. She always woke up early in the morning and went to practice at the arena in school before everyone else awakened.

Her determination and willingness to learn pushed her to becoming one of the best figure skaters in the campus.

Neva's talent was unmatched and everyone who saw her on the ice would be overcome by intense emotions. She had a way of provoking people's feelings by merely skating.

Some would cheer happily and others would cheer while crying—it didn't matter to her as long as she was feeling appreciated. She always embraced an attitude of gratitude.

"Neva, when will you come home?" His father would ask all the time whenever they talked on the phone.

"Soon!" She'd reply as she cut off the call to go back to rehearsals.

She had let figure skating take control of her whole being and now she had become one with the sport.

After a few years, she joined the Olympics in Tokyo that would be held in a year.

She decided to go back to her hometown to visit her father and tell him about the good news. But as she arrived, she found him bedridden.

"Papa, why didn't you tell me you were sick?" She asked.

"He has been sick for months," her father's caretaker earnestly explained.

"I didn't want to make you worry," George added.

"Of course I'd worry, since you're my father and I love you. very much," Neva whispered as she began to sob.

Even though she seemed tough on the outside, she had the most compassionate heart.

"Don't cry, my girl. Everything will be alright, you'll see!" Her father assured.

So Neva made a key decision to put Swan Lake on hold to cater to her father. She also decided to help the community by teaching figure skating at the arena she used to practice at when she was just a girl. The children loved her since she was patient and understanding while teaching them. She also made sure her father was alright and took care of him.

After a few months, her father died and she had to go back to the city. Throughout her life, she had never felt the kind of heaviness she was feeling. It was as if it was pulling her down. Guilt further crowded her mind and she started practicing Ice skating every time she had the chance to—she couldn't rest even for a second because if she rested, she would think and if she thought, she would feel deep sadness.

Before her father died, he'd given her his blessing and allowed her to figure skate, but still she was overcome by sadness.

She was never late during the rehearsals and always gave it her all. Whatever the coach would suggest, she would gladly agree even though some of the moves would hurt her feet.

This time she wasn't enjoying figure skating. Instead, she was punishing herself by using the sport because she felt responsible for her father's demise. He formerly had been calling her and she was too busy for him.

On a fateful night, as everyone was asleep, Neva woke up and sat by the window.

She looked at the sky, but the city lights were too bright, and so she couldn't see the stars. The moon shone alone in the pitch-black sky.

"I wish to find peace and gratitude again in my life," Neva politely asked.

The same star that was brighter than the rest twinkled alone in the dark sky. Not long after, she fell asleep. That night she dreamt of her mother and the next day, she signed up for therapy and started as soon as possible.

While at the therapist's office, she explained that the past had clung on to her and she wanted to forgive herself and stay in the present moment. Since the Olympics were coming soon, she wanted to conquer her mental problems.

"I'll tell you a short story," the therapist said. "A red cardinal was sitting on a tree reflecting on life. He was grateful and content with life. He enjoyed the silence, and thought about how wonderful his life had been and how all the struggles he had gone through made him grow as an individual. "Now more than ever, I understand the little things in life are all that matters," he cheerfully confessed.

"Krrrrr-Krrrrr!" the hornbill screeched. He was flying towards the red cardinal.

I'm trying to enjoy my silence. However, the Hornbill is ruining that for me. Nonetheless, I won't get angry because he probably has a good explanation for what the ruckus is all about, The red cardinal thought to himself.

"Good morning Mr. Red," the Hornbill greeted the red cardinal.

"I'm alright, but If I may ask, why are you making so much noise early this morning?" Mr. Red politely inquired.

"Oh! I'm sorry, Mr. Red, bu-bu-but, I don't have food for my family," the hornbill chirped as he sank in disappointment.

"Oh! I see, I'm sorry!" The red cardinal replied.

Hornbill's expression displayed deep sorrow.

"Hmmm, I might have an idea!" The red cardinal proposed, stroking his chin.

The Hornbill jumped in amazement. "Really Mr. Red?" He couldn't conceal his excitement.

"Yes, I might have some extra worms for you and your family," The red cardinal confirmed.

"Thank you so much! I truly appreciate having a friend like you, Mr. Red," the Hornbill happily cheeped.

They both flew away merrily. The red cardinal practiced Mindfulness. He didn't let his outer experiences dictate his mood. He knew what was happening around him; however, he responded wisely. Mindfulness is the act of responding wisely to the things that happen to you without judgment. Mindfulness begins with understanding. The red cardinal didn't judge the Hornbill by the noise he was making, he also didn't let anger dictate his emotions.

On the contrary, he chose understanding. What you choose to focus on grows; it all starts with your mind. The red cardinal planted seeds of understanding and cultivated mindfulness.

"The story is nice, but I really don't understand where you're going with this," Neva explained.

"In order to let go of the past, you need to stay in the present moment. You need to stop letting external factors have an impact on your life," the therapist added.

At first, she didn't understand what the therapist was trying to convey but after a few more sessions, she decided to live like the cardinal. She stopped judging herself and instead forgave and understood herself, removing a heavy load off her shoulders. She further cultivated an attitude of gratitude.

She resumed practicing Ice skating, but this time she was cheery than usual and had fun during practice because she wasn't too focused on the past or future, she was enjoying the present moment.

Swan Lake was a transformative piece for her. In Neva's mind, she had to let go of the Odile in her and embrace the Odette in her, becoming a better person with each passing day.

Soon she flew to Tokyo for the competition and the day of the performance arrived.

The audience started arriving to watch the contestants. After a while, everyone arrived and sat patiently in the hall, waiting for the show to start.

It began and Neva was the last to be called on stage.

She patiently waited for her turn. Her makeup, costume, and stance were so captivating, special, and beautiful.

Her name was called out. Piano music filled the room and her body fell into routine.

At this moment, she exemplified the Black Swan and skated skilfully. The audience was silent, as they all paid close attention to her. The rush of excitement that she was feeling was unimaginable. She also cherished an attitude of gratitude in the here and now!

After her performance as the Black Swan; Odile, she transformed to a white swan; Odette and she offered her all, as she felt the wind, the energy of the dance; it was though she became one with the White Swan!

As she made her final twirl and the music reached an end, the audience applauded as she skated from the arena. All contestants assembled in the arena, so the judges could proudly announce the winner.

In the end, Neva wasn't the 1st or 2nd runner up; instead, she won the Olympics.

As she was admiring her trophy she whispered, "Thank you stars, this is for you mom and dad!"

Learned lessons

All in all, as this clever and informative tale with Neva suggests, you must never allow your external situation to ever make you react poorly. Instead, you should stay in the present moment and mindfully focus on what you still have. You can use this mindset for bereavement, loss, optimism, school, sports, and friendships.

When we stay in the present moment, we can engage with our senses. We can also learn to embrace an attitude of gratitude.

Specifically, gratitude allows us to break the ice and excel at whatever you choose. We can also be grateful, even when time gets tough, stressful, or uncertain. An attitude of gratitude is like a crown or a sparkling tiara.

Skate with grace and gratitude in the present as you complete some post-reading fun below:

1. Gratitude Box: Make a box and add 2-4 items that symbolize what/who you're grateful for.

2. Star Breathing: Try star breathing, affirmations, meditating, or yoga to stay in the present this week. Did any of these activities help? Why? How?

3. Picture Perfect: Which scene would you like to draw, sketch, or paint? Try your hand at bringing it to life now.

4. Swan Lake Break: With an adult's permission, go online and discover 2-4 fun facts about this performance. You may also check out a book about the topic at your local library.

5. Life After Loss: Create a card, poem, or letter for anyone that you've lost. Maybe it's a pet?

CONCLUSION

Thank you sincerely for reading and growing together in this charming compilation. Always remember to step into and show your own *girl power* hour 24/7, so you can shine and soar each day with confidence, pride, and commitment.

When you meet with any challenge or obstacle in life, remember this creative and courageous cast of global, strong, gutsy, and diverse female characters. You can use them as motivation and muses on your own journey to become more empowered, focused, present, successful, and supported.

Plus, you can now proactively review, apply, and share all the amazing life lessons that you've acquired from these terrific tales. Your newfound knowledge justice, grit, work/school/sports/life balance, resilience, determination, gender equity, an attitude of gratitude, discipline, fairness, perseverance, optimism, anti-bullying, coping with family illness, loss, and bereavement, maintaining a clear focus and concentration, body positivity, breaking stereotypes, self-belief, self-confidence, problem solving skills, the value of teamwork, forgiveness, and other key concepts will allow you to shimmer, glimmer, and shine! These core character education lessons will be your superpowers as you navigate through life, sports, school, family, friendships, and strife.

Aside from all the insights about girl power galore, you've also mastered and gained so much cultural and geographical information related to renowned and special places such as the Swiss Alps, the Outer Banks, Kentucky, North Carolina, Los Angeles and San Diego, The Florida Keys, Bali, Indonesia, Omaha, Nebraska, California, Arizona, Delaware, England, Massachusetts, Tokyo, Japan, and other memorable settings through these terrific tales. Feel free to re-read them and do the exercises to keep your skills sharp. Glow and go from East to West!

Lastly, glow and show *girl power for hours* as you start to follow the stories' main characters when you splash, climb, throw, skate, catch, shoot, and spring about the world of sports-your way today!

Thank You

Thank you very much for picking up a copy of my book.

You could have chosen from a variety of different books, but you decided to take a chance and go with this one. so, thank you for purchasing this book and reading on it to the conclusion.

Before you leave, I'd like to request a tiny favor from you. Could you please consider leaving an Amazon review? The greatest and simplest way to promote independent authors like me is to write a review. Your input will assist me in continuing to write the types of books that will assist you in achieving the results you desire. It would mean a lot to me if you could let me know your opinion.

Made in the USA
Monee, IL
16 September 2024

65976024R00069